I0485694

Beautiful Circles 2 Coloring Book

by Artist
Dwyanna Stoltzfus

Join the Fun!!
Share your colored pages!!

You are invited to color the pages
From this and all publications by
Dwyanna Stoltzfus. Then scan and post
Your colored creations in
Coloring with Dwyanna
Adult Coloring Group
On facebook
https://web.facebook.com/groups/1519357628356169/?_rdr
Join Coloring with Dwyanna Coloring Group,
And have fun sharing your colored pages
And meeting new coloring friends.
Members of the group will also have access
To free coloring pages.
You are welcome to share your colored pages on
Any social network, make sure to mention the title of
The book and the author/artist name.
Uncolored images may not be shared.

Check out my blog at:

coloringwithdwyanna.blogspot.com7

PDF Printable coloring pages available

On Etsy at

https://www.etsy.com/people/dwyannastoltzfus

Follow Dwyanna's art on facebook at

Oodles of Doodles Designs –

Adult Coloring Books by

Dwyanna Stoltzfus

https://web.facebook.com/Oodles-of-Doodles-Designs-Adult-Coloring-

Books-by-Dwyanna-Stoltzfus-743502922387046/

About

You are going to love this book!!

This coloring book is for anyone who loves to color!!

Beginner colorist and even children will enjoy the bold beautiful illustrations.

This color book has the exact drawings as the Beautiful Circles 2 Mini Coloring Book,

only these are on a larger scale making them easy for children and adults

who prefer a more simple design with heavy black lines to enjoy.

You can even pair up with your children if you like.

Many adults often enjoy the more intricate details of the Beautiful Circles 2 Mini Book,

now your children can color with you, coloring the same picture in this

full size version. This coloring book will provide many hours of fun,

entertainment. It will also provide hours of peaceful calm and relaxation.

Coloring is highly recommended for both children and adults.

We encourage our precious children to draw and color as a relaxing quiet activity.

Coloring can have the same relaxing/calming effect on adults.

It is especially beneficial to those who struggle with anxiety or stress.

It's the perfect stress relief.

In this coloring book you will find 52 bold and beautiful illustrations, printed

one per page. A collection of 52 stunning images inspired by doodle art.

You will find beautiful intricate flowers, swirls, and many detailed

doodle patterns. You can use this coloring book for a quiet activity for your

children or to help you relax and unwind or just to have fun.

You can color the illustrations simply or add depth by shading.

Crayons can be used in this book as well as gel pens, markers, and colored pencils.

Get ready to color 52 Beautiful Circles full of doodle

art designs by Artist Dwyanna Stoltzfus.

Acknowledgments

Thank You to my family for all your support of my

Art and this project. I could not have done it without you!!

Thank You God for the gift and love

Of art and drawing!!

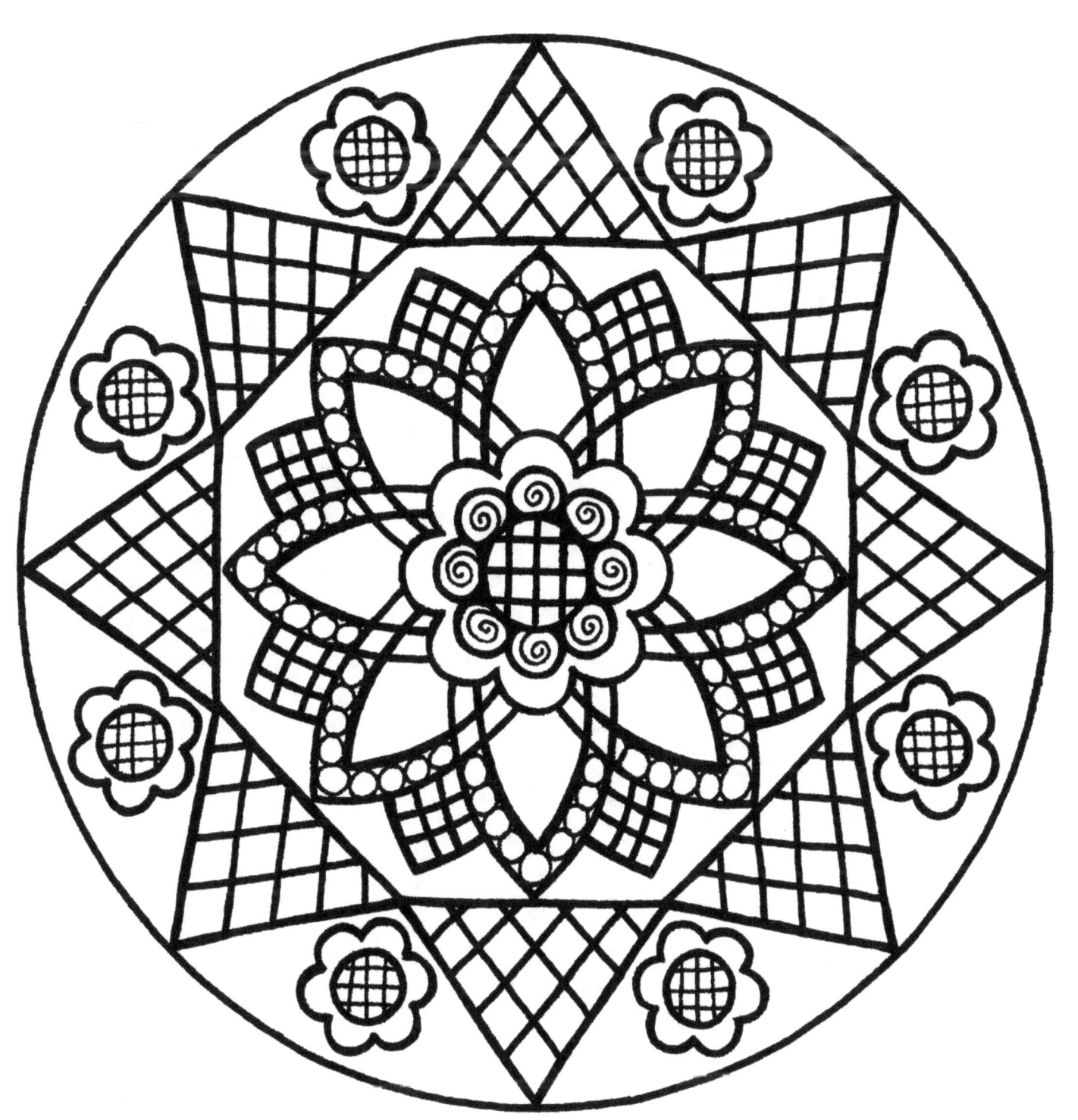

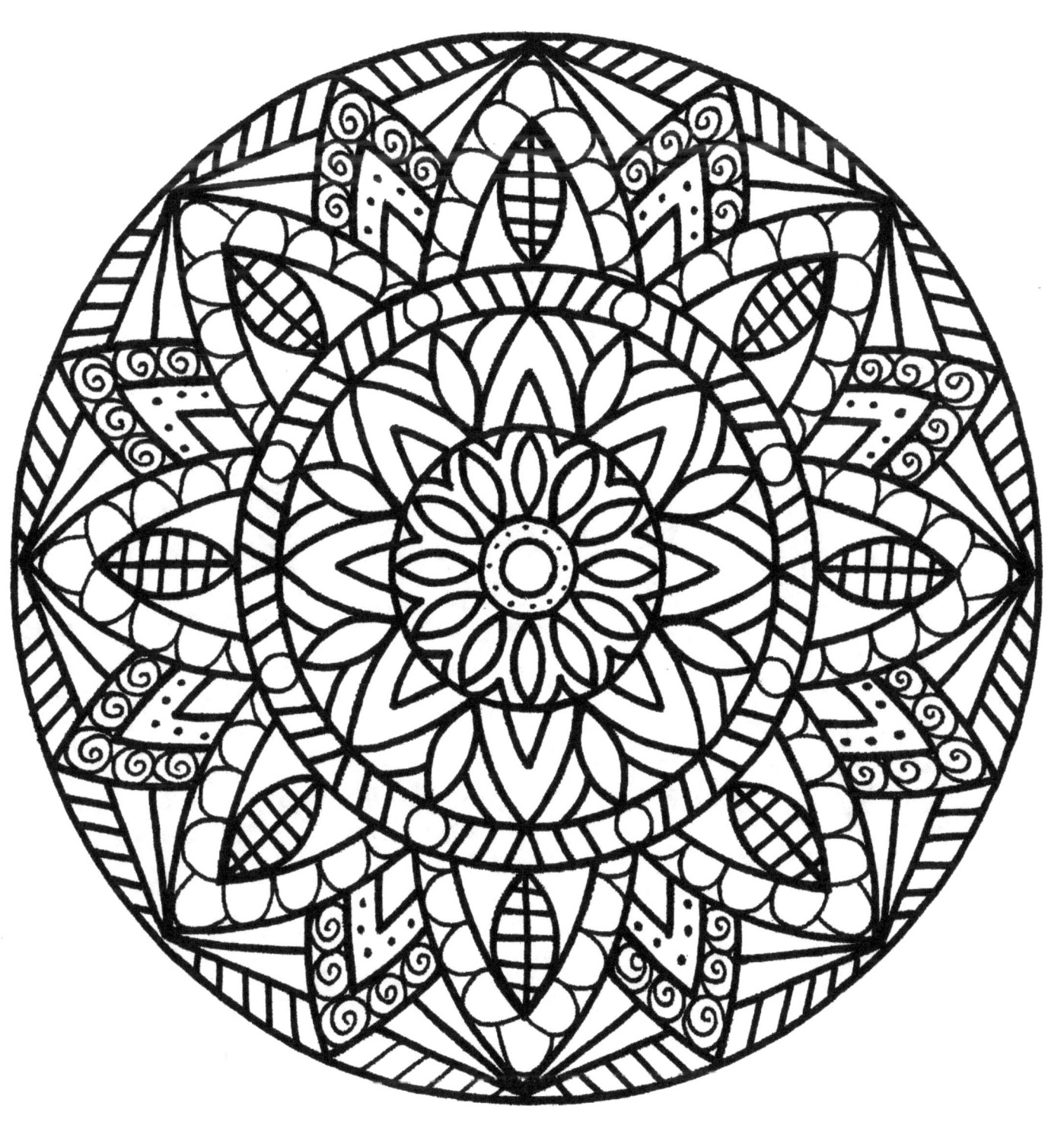

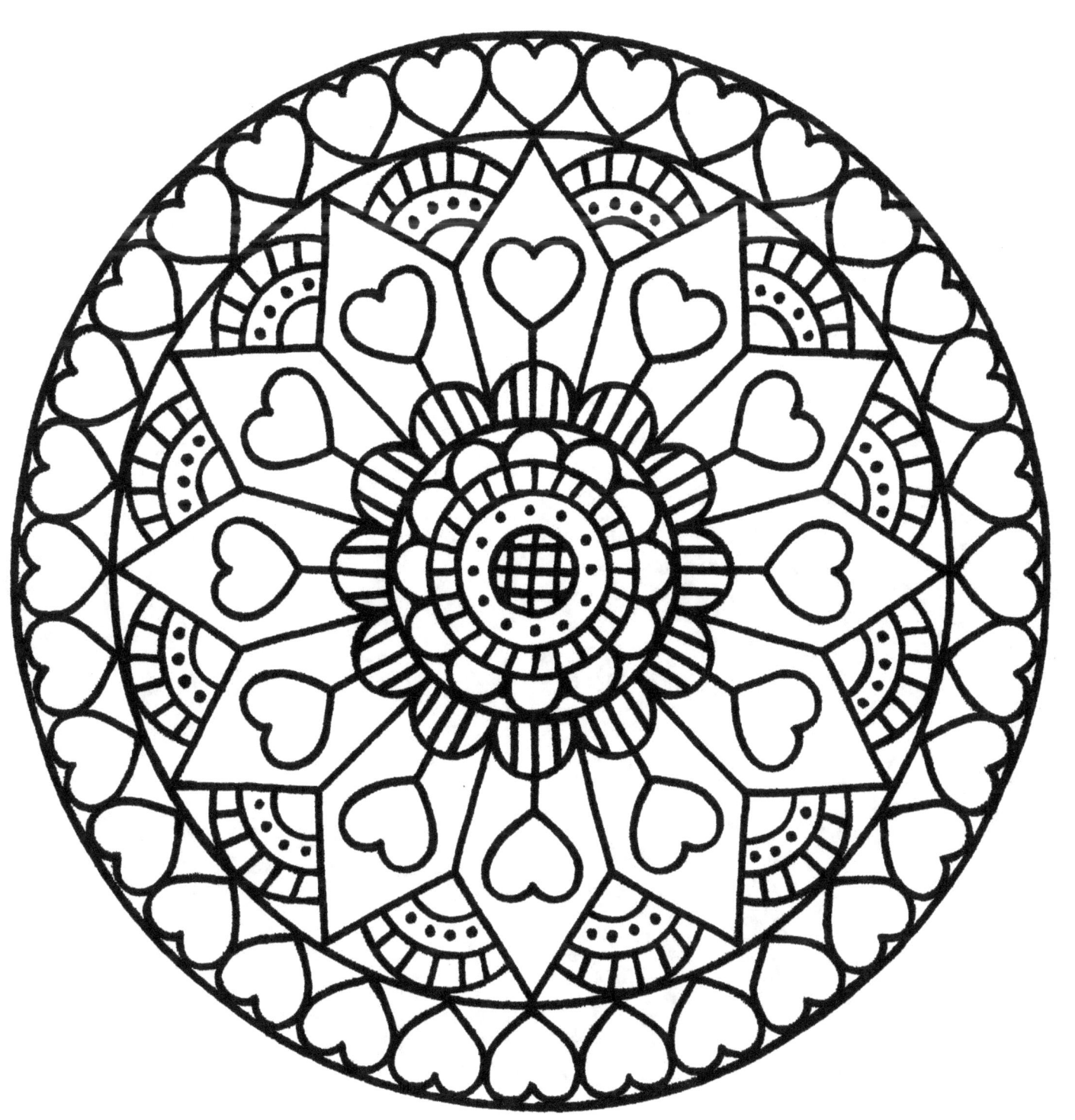

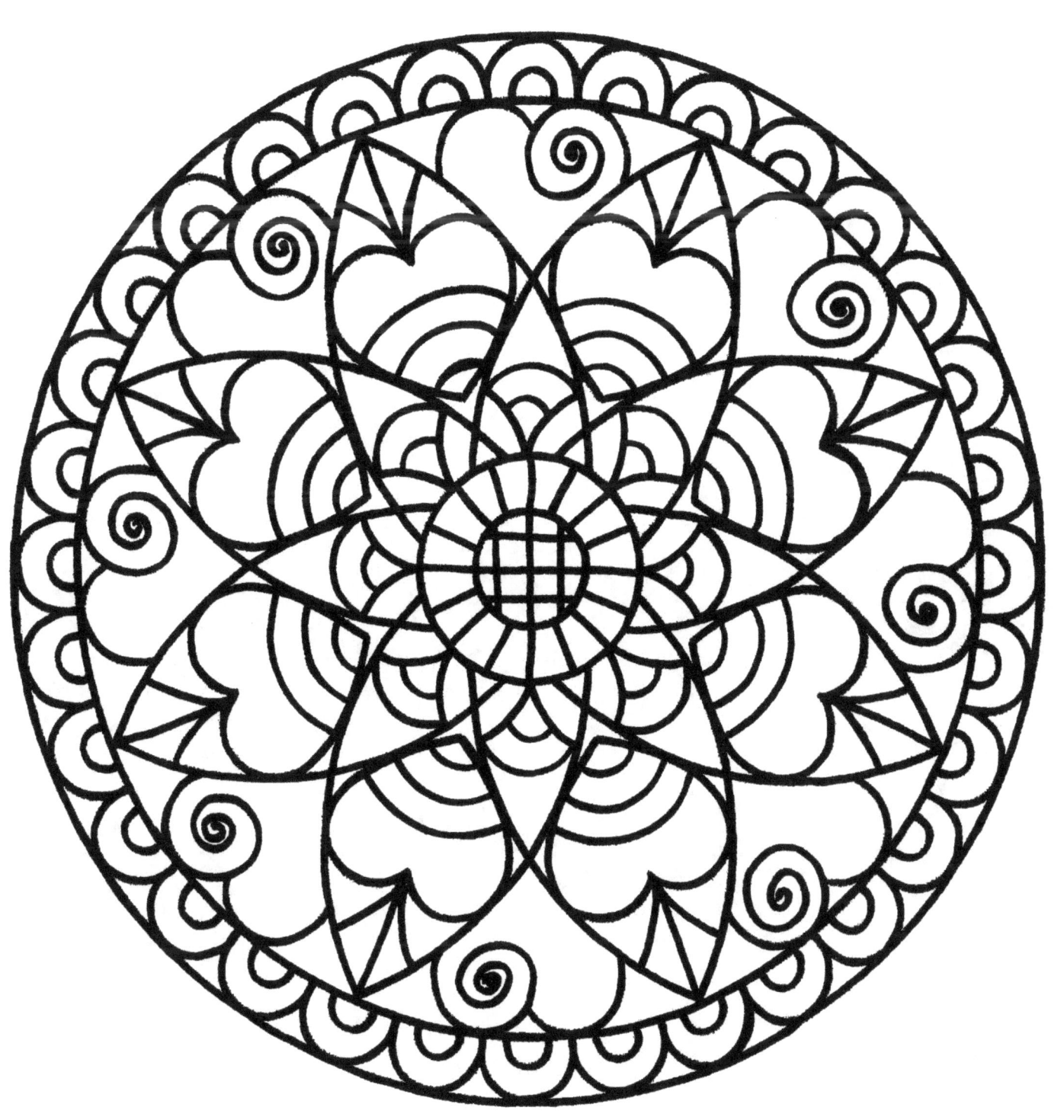

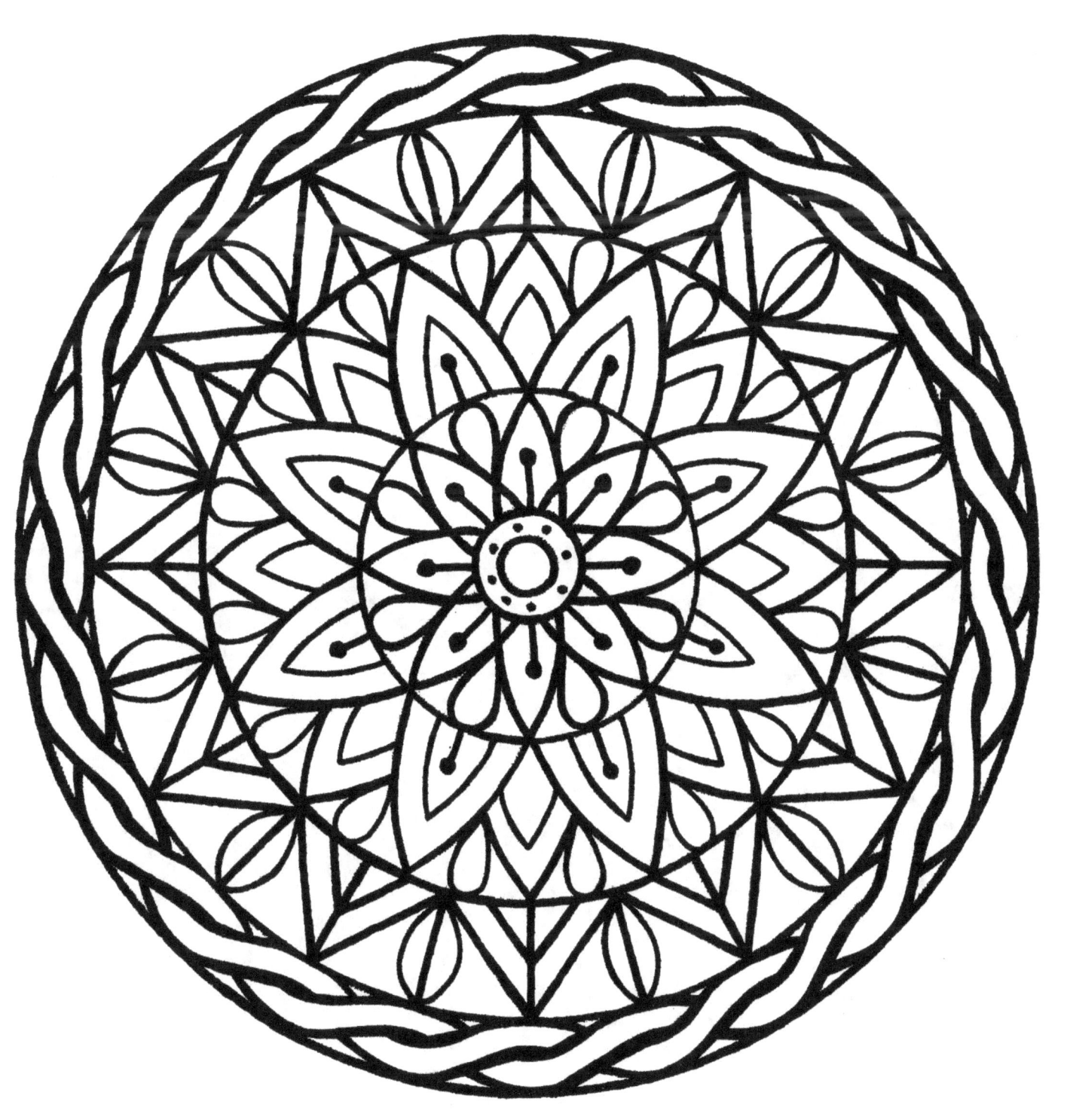

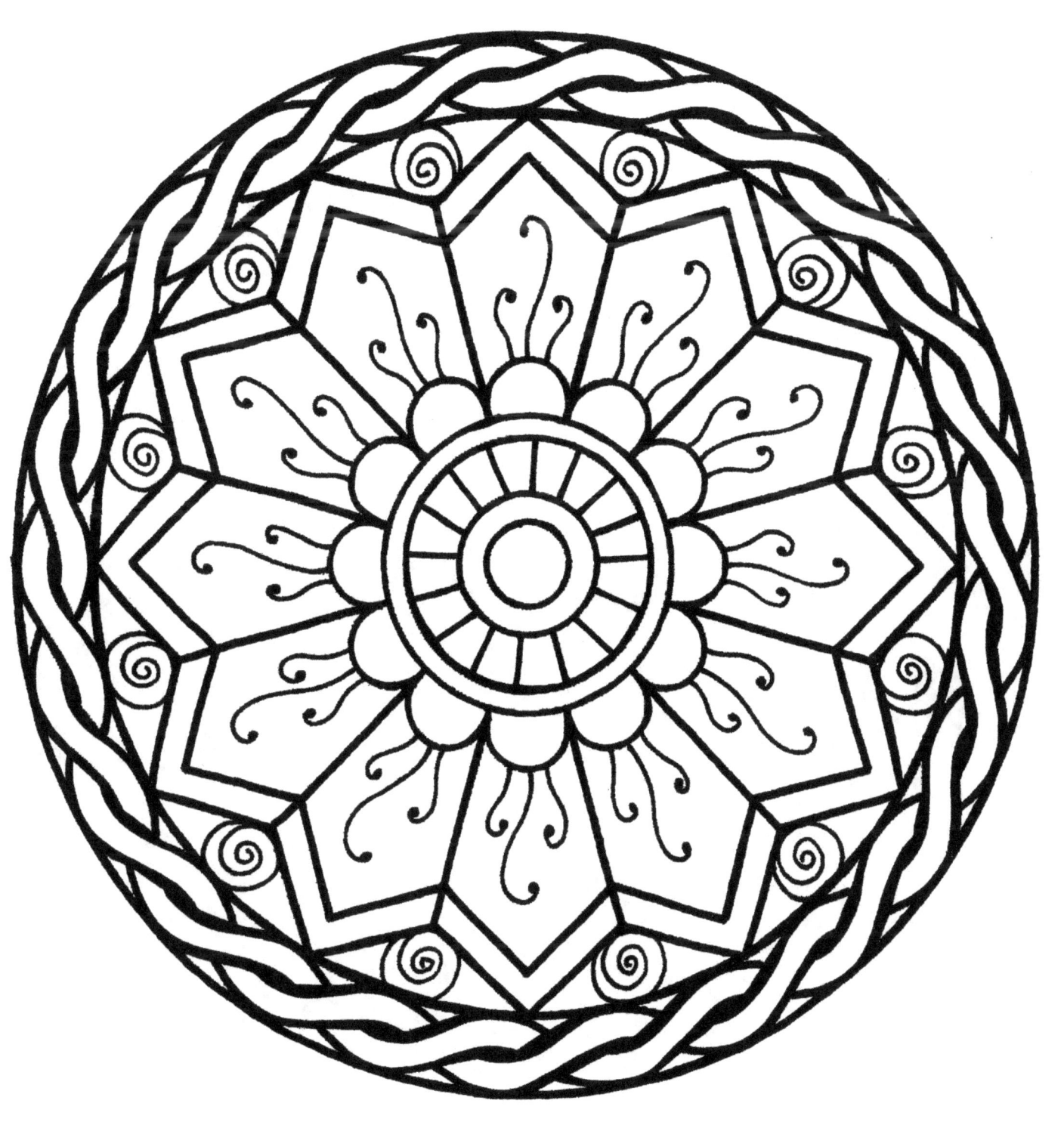

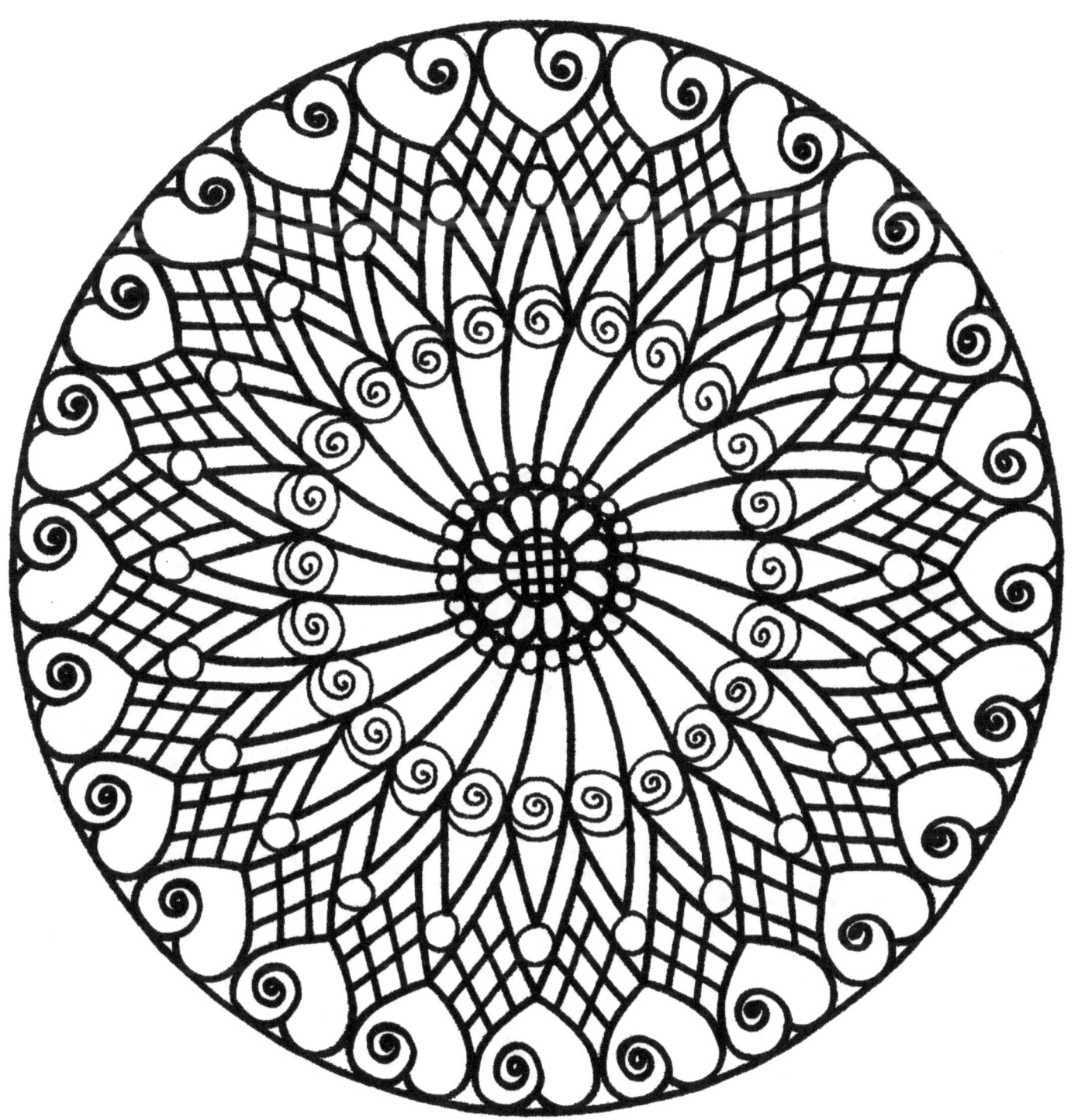

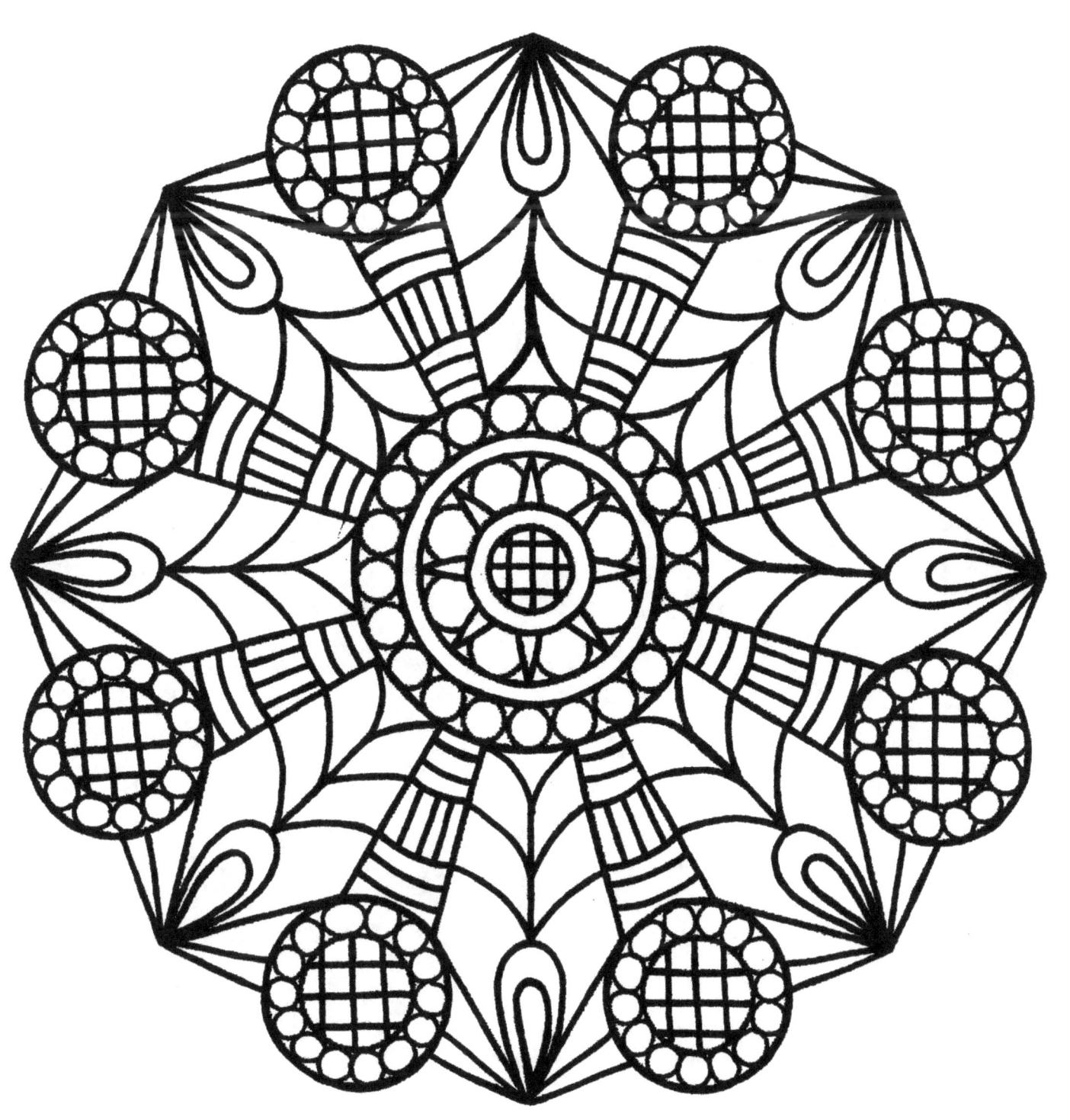

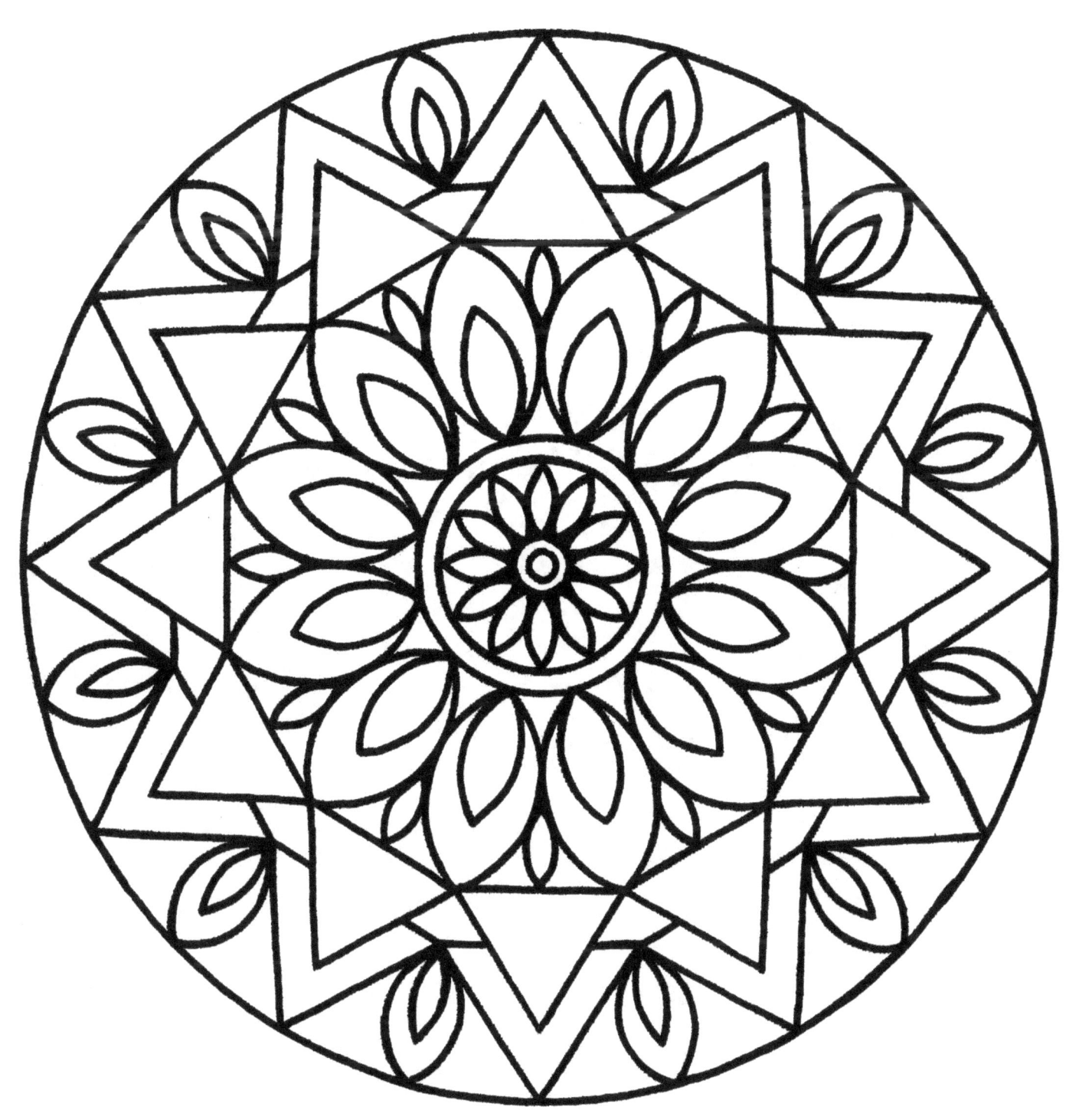

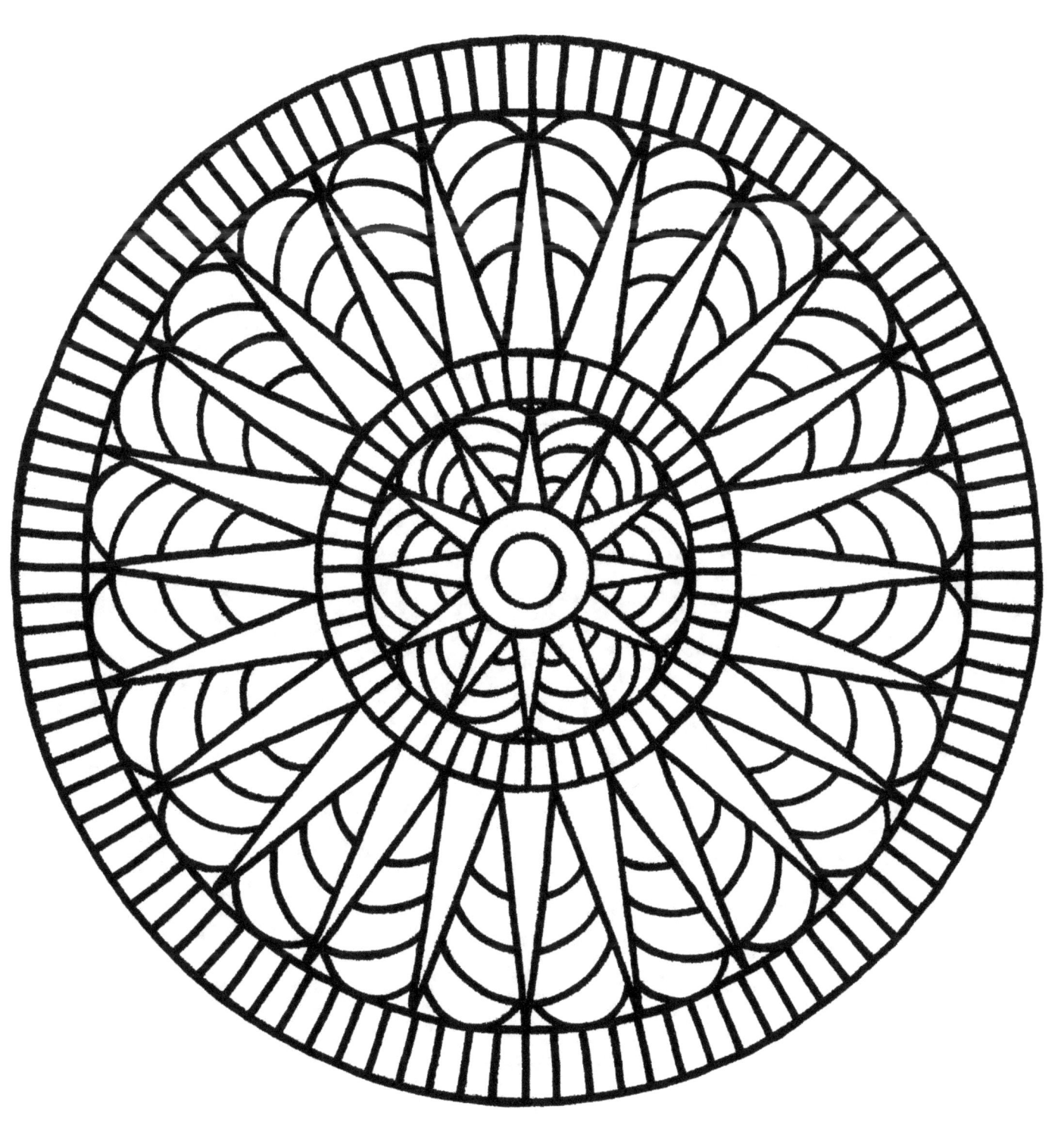

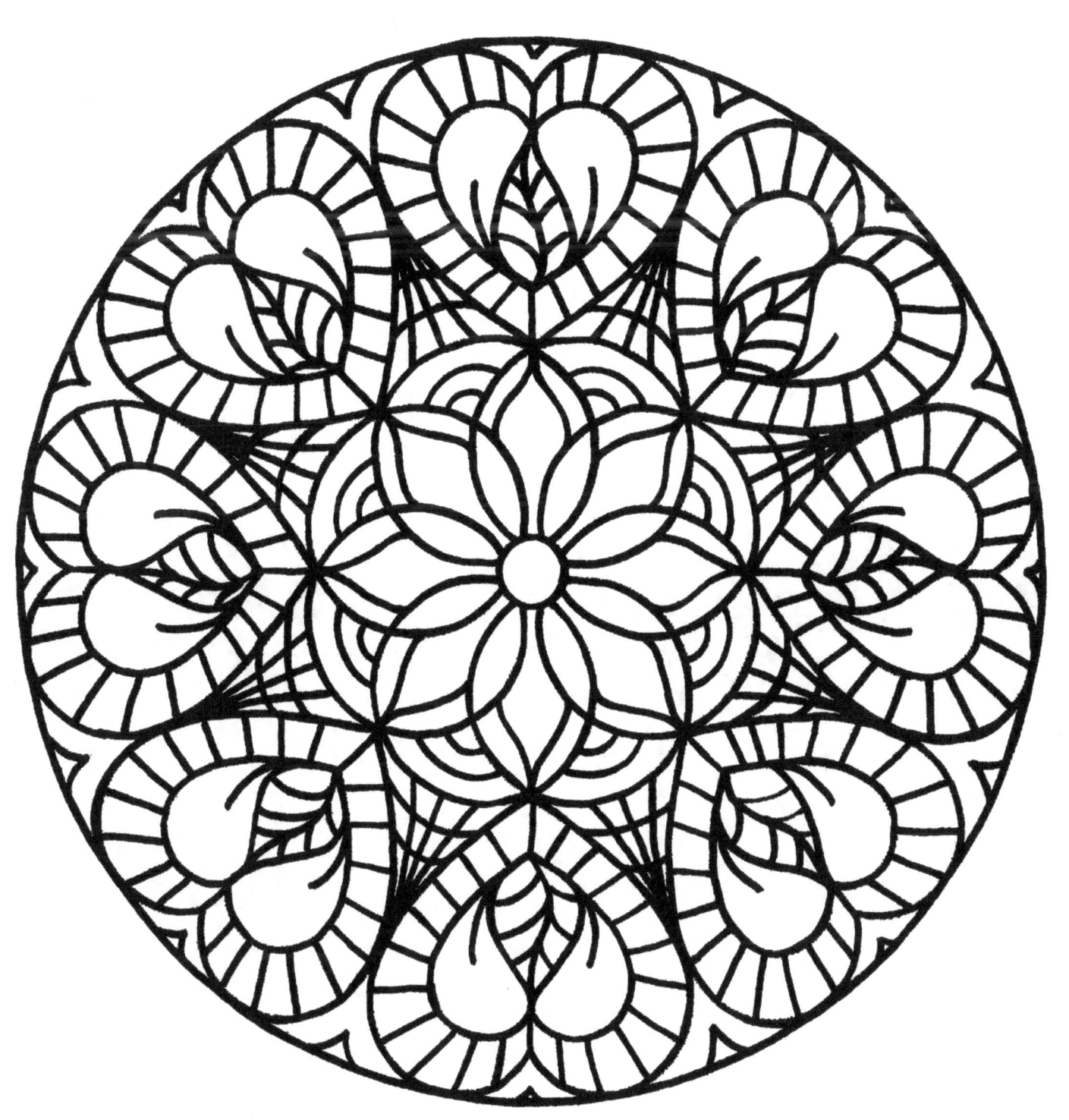

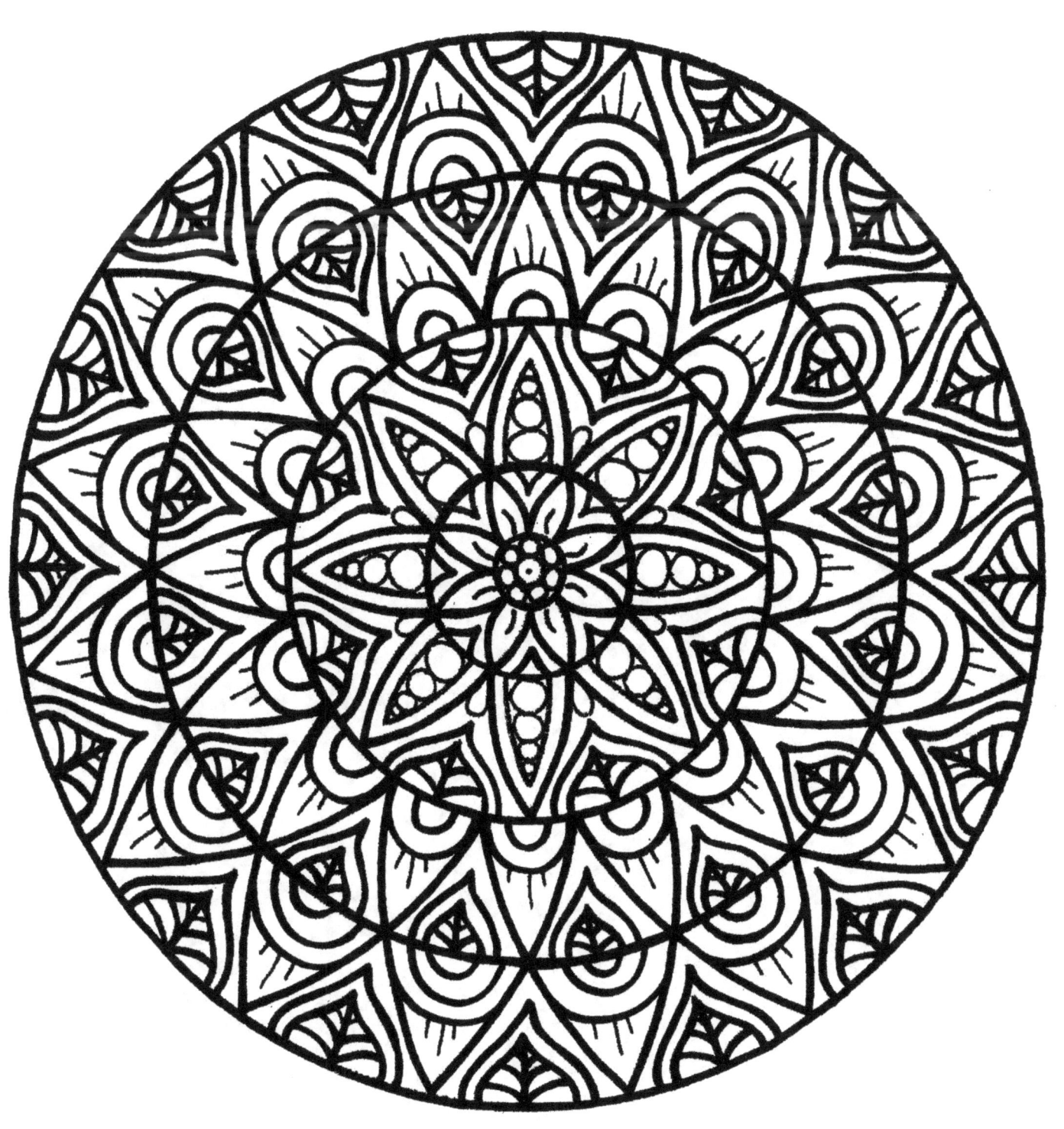

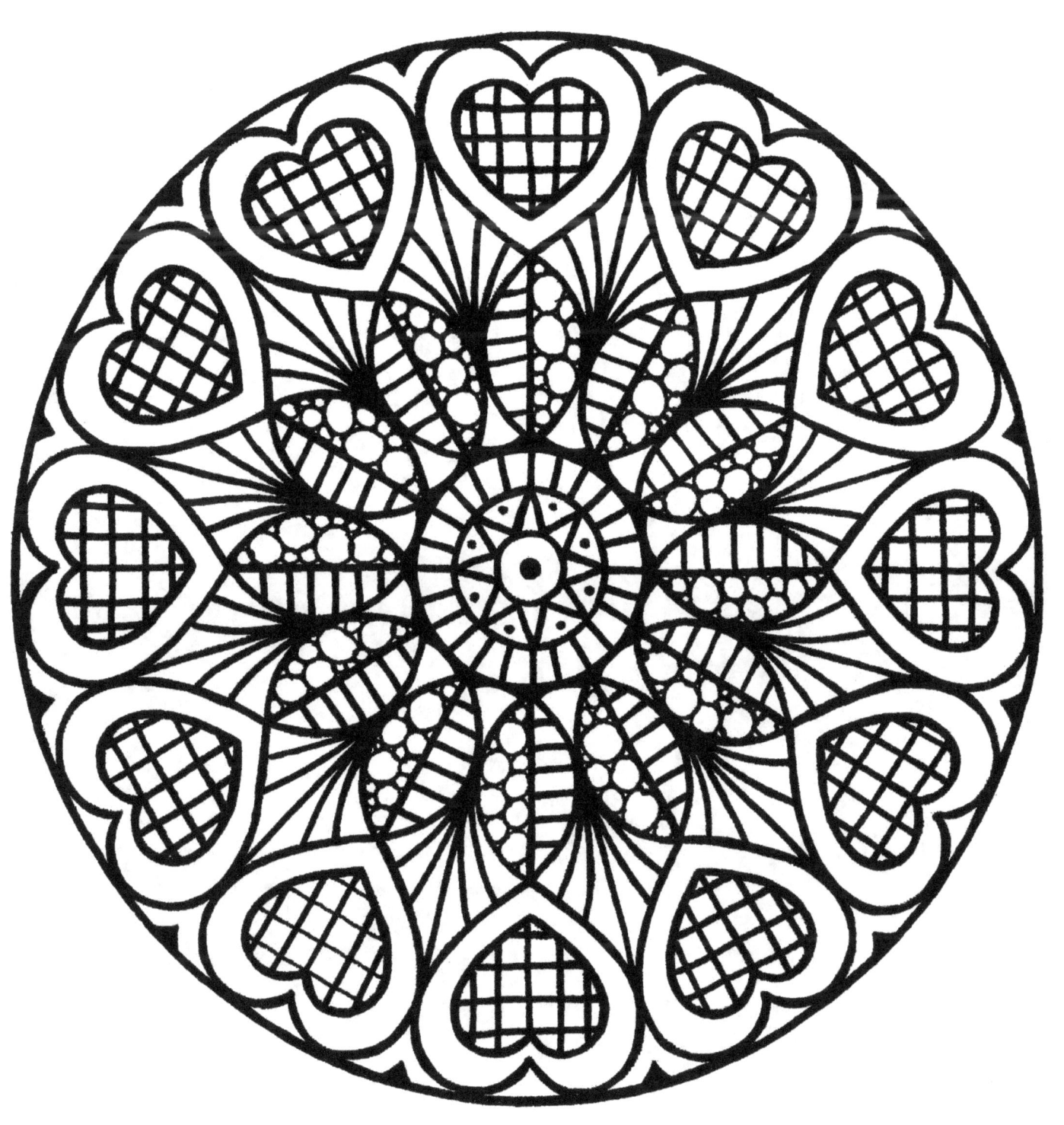

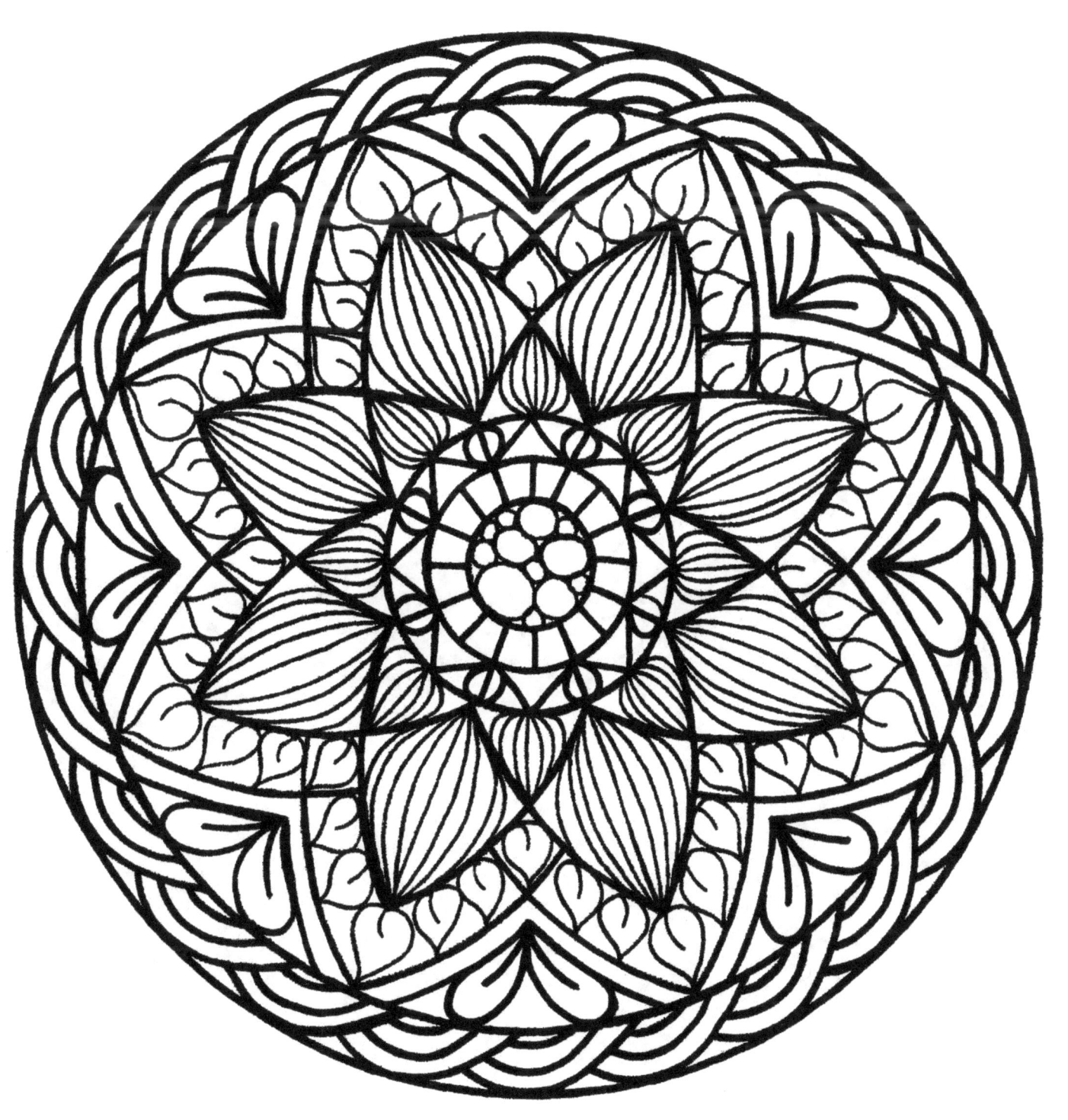

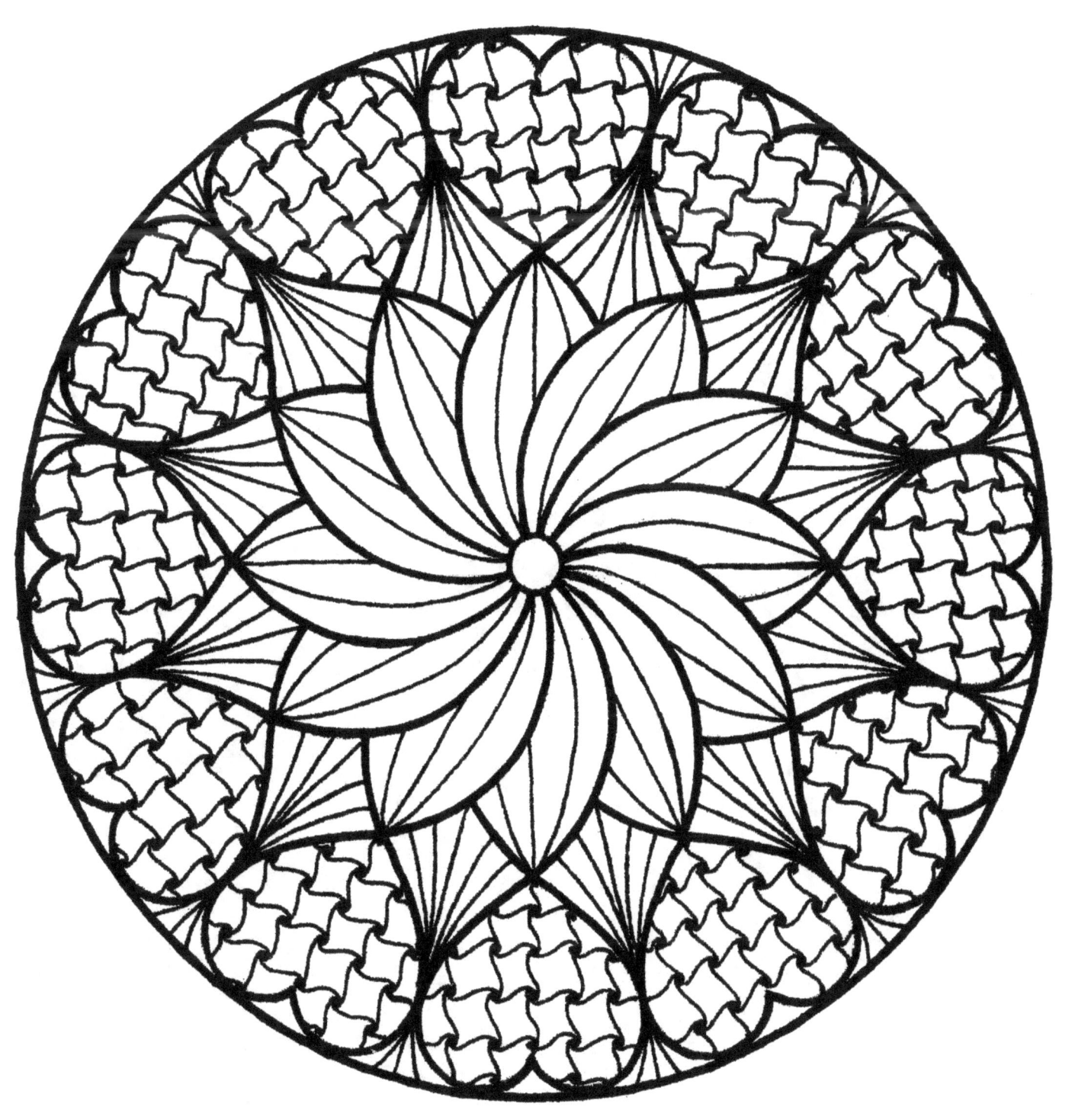

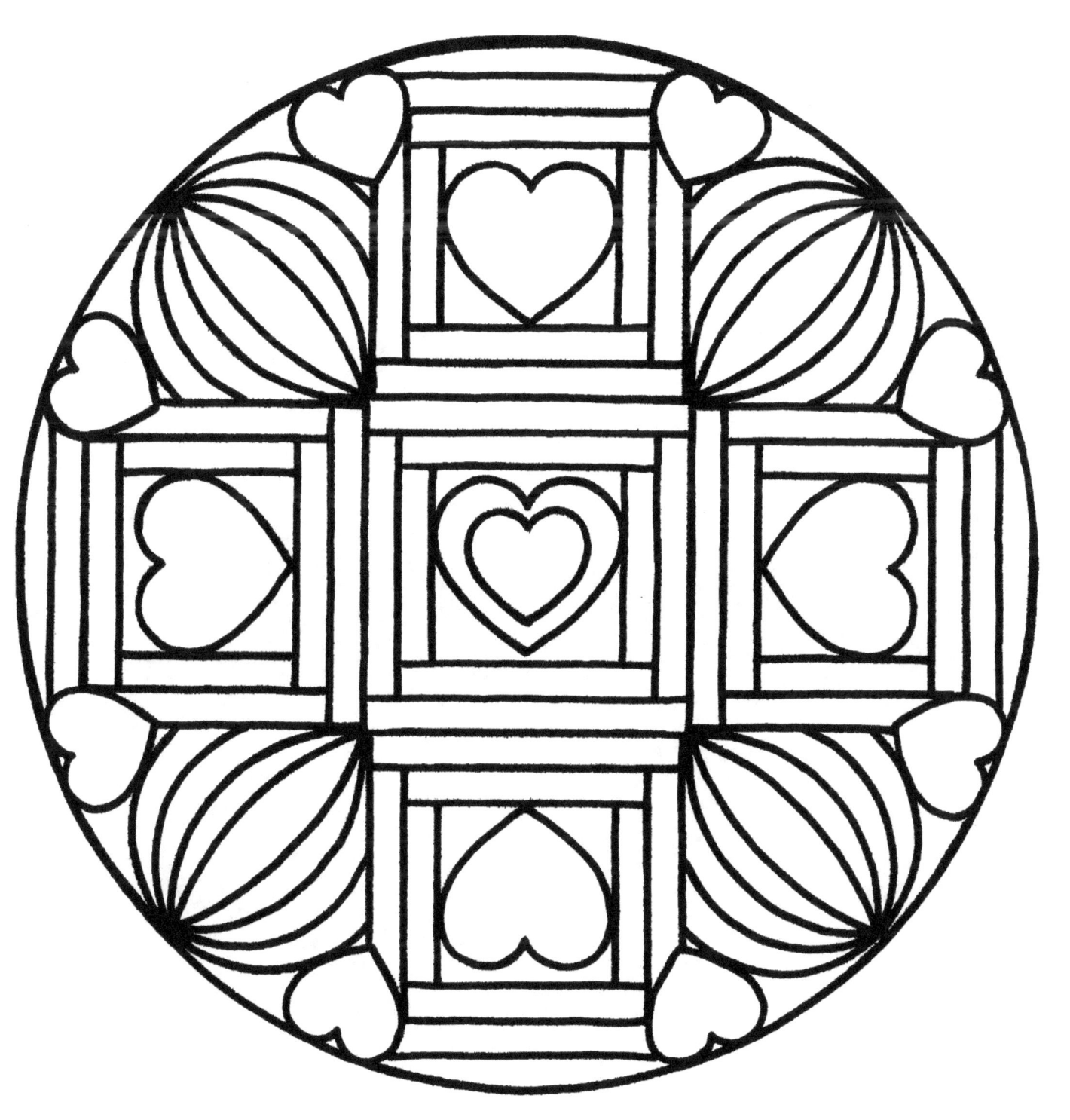

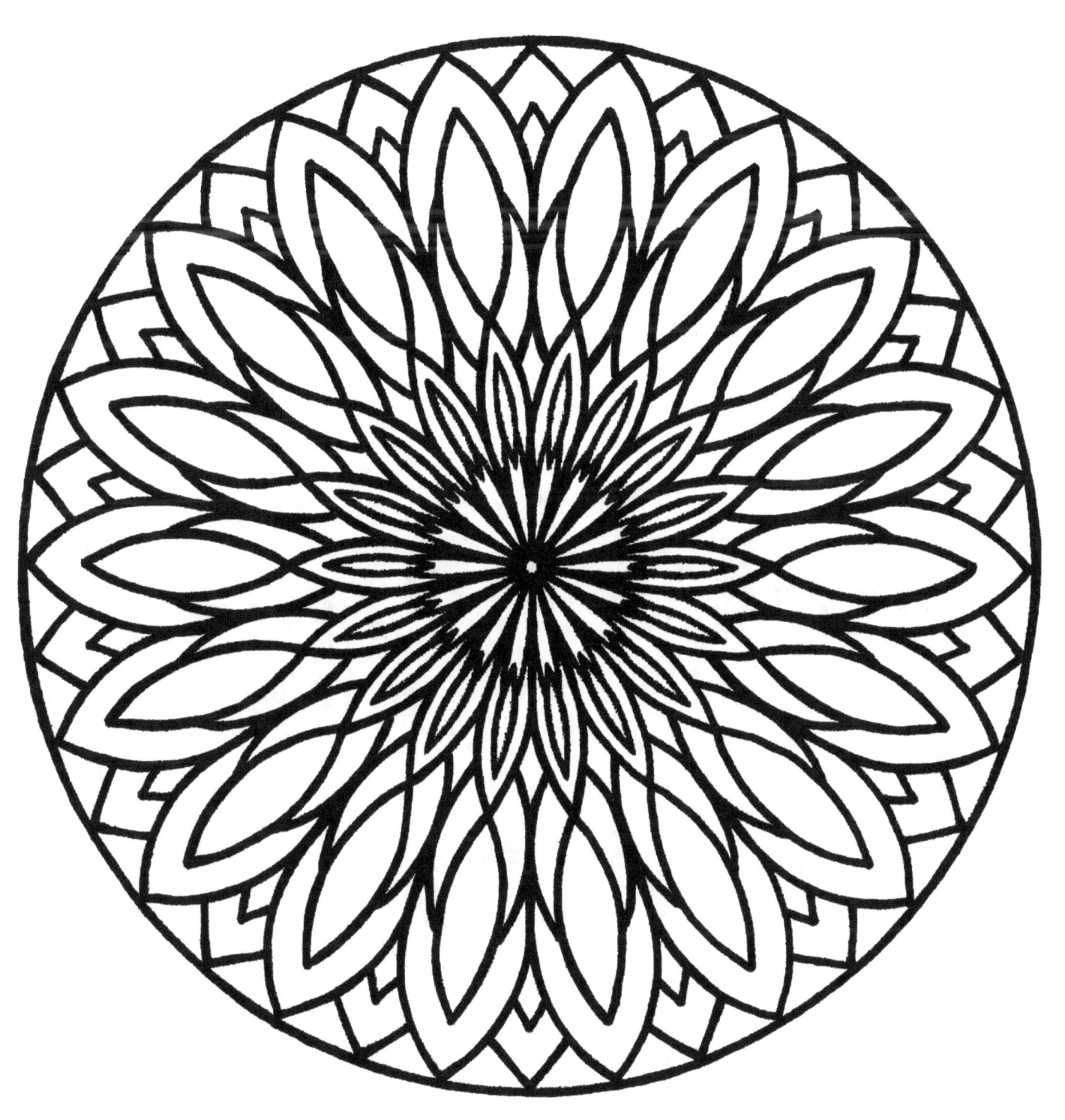

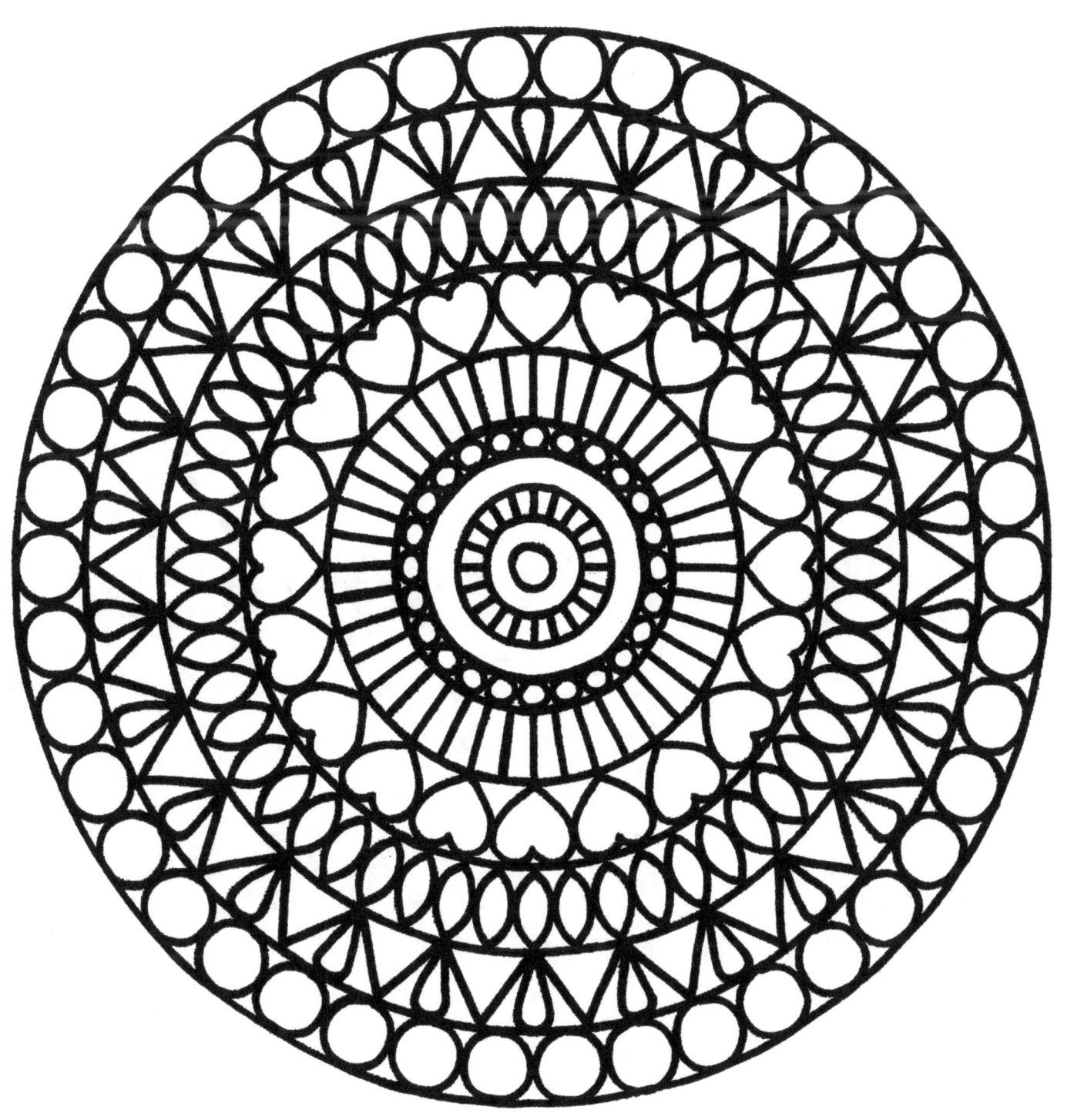

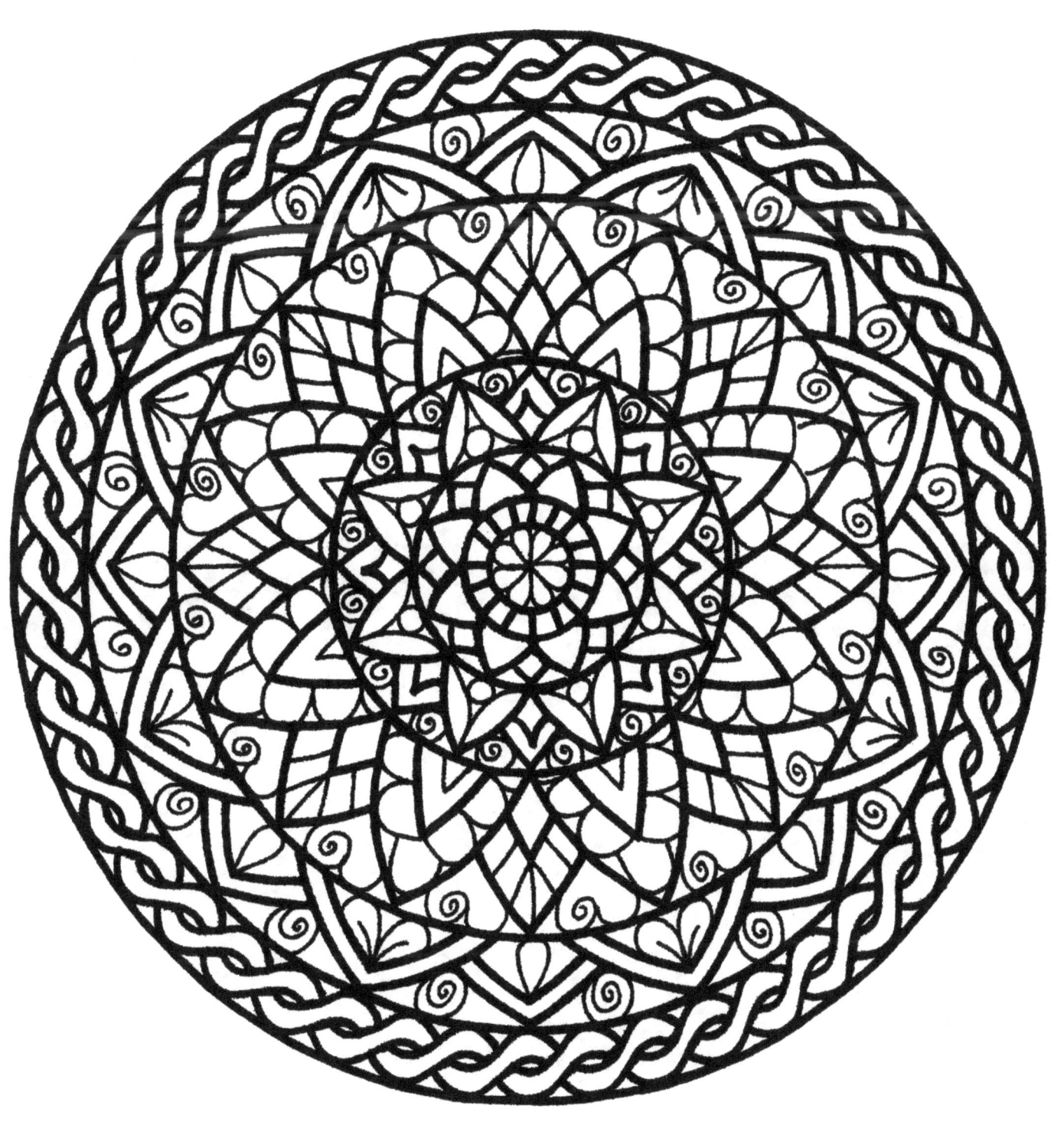

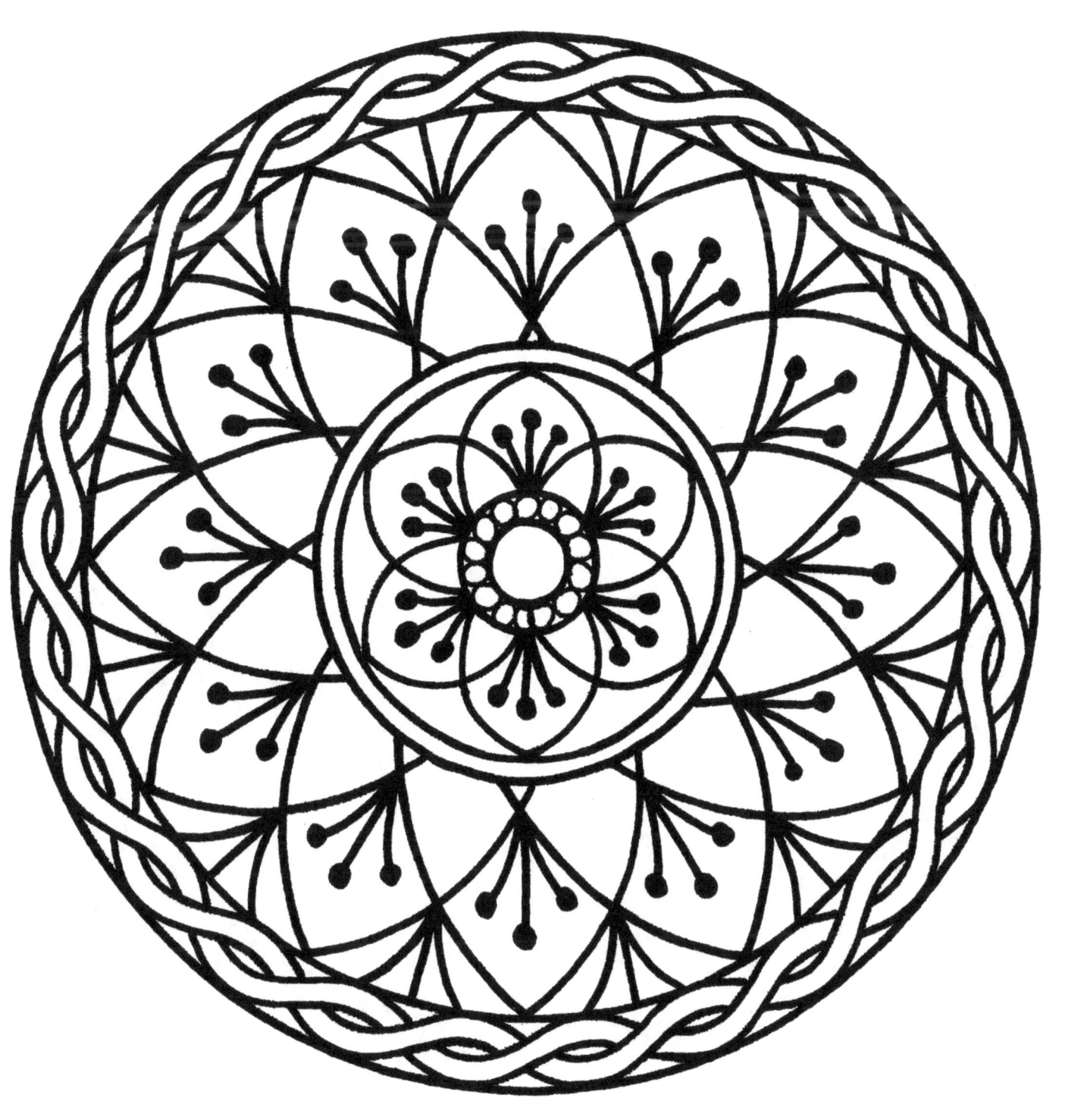

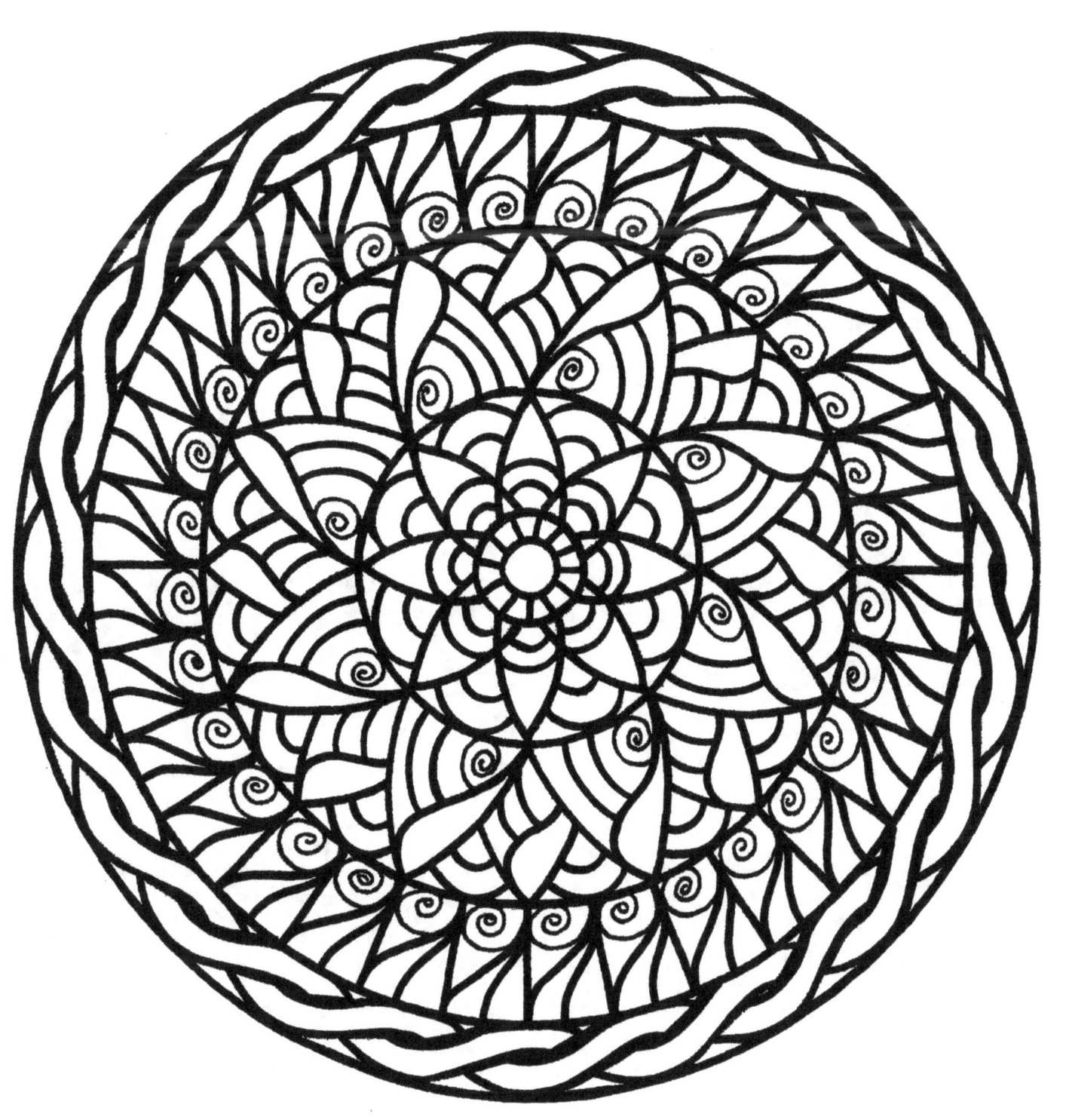

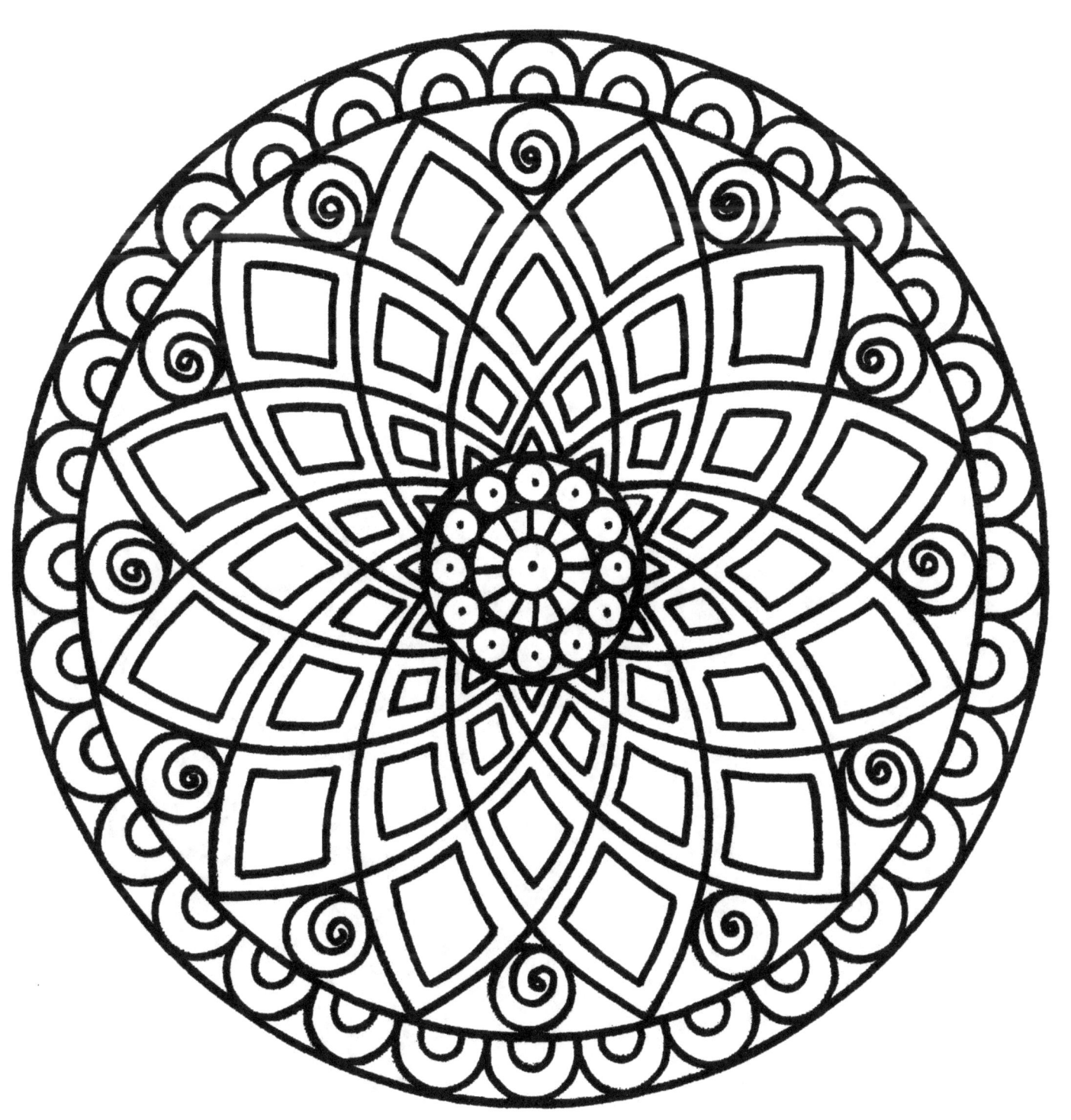

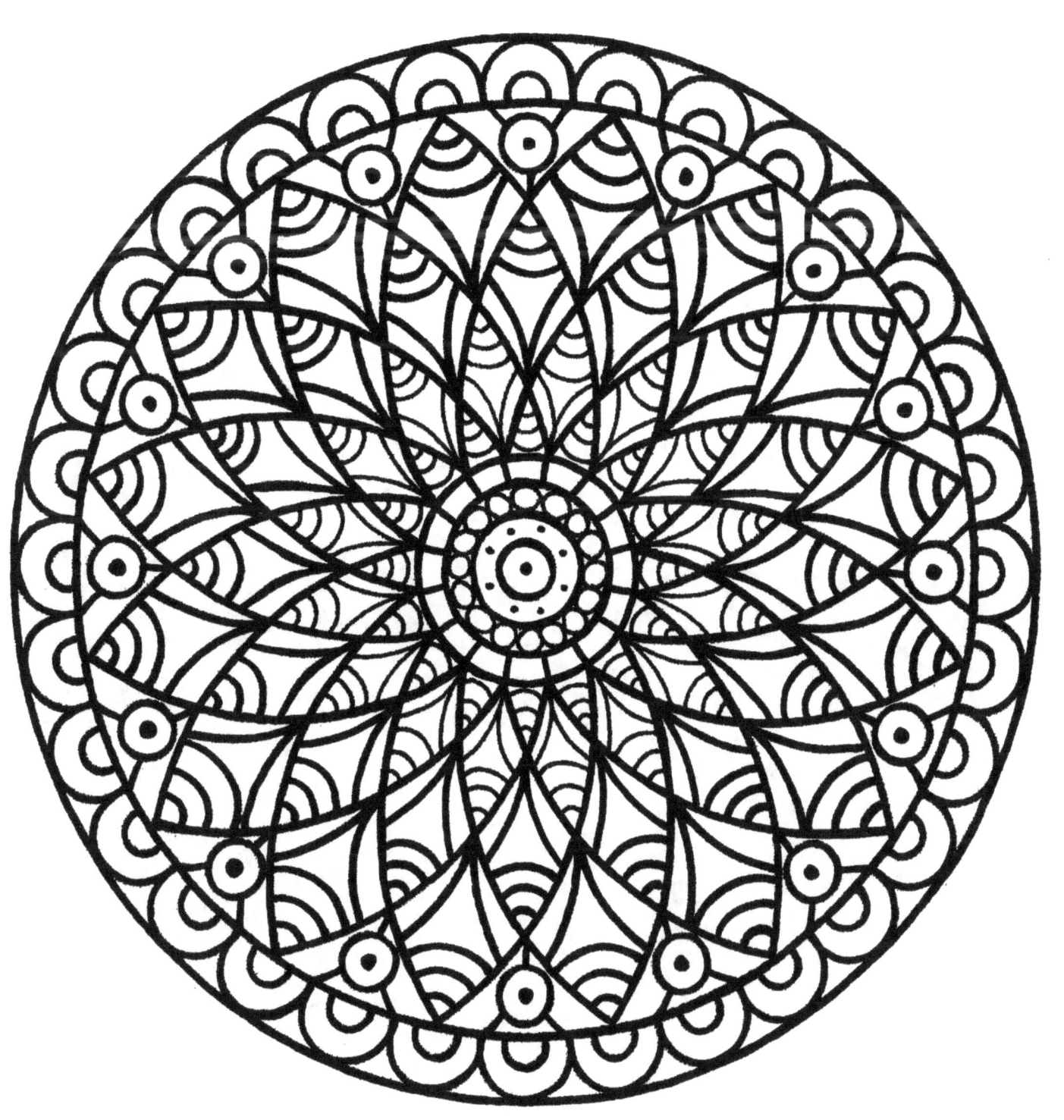

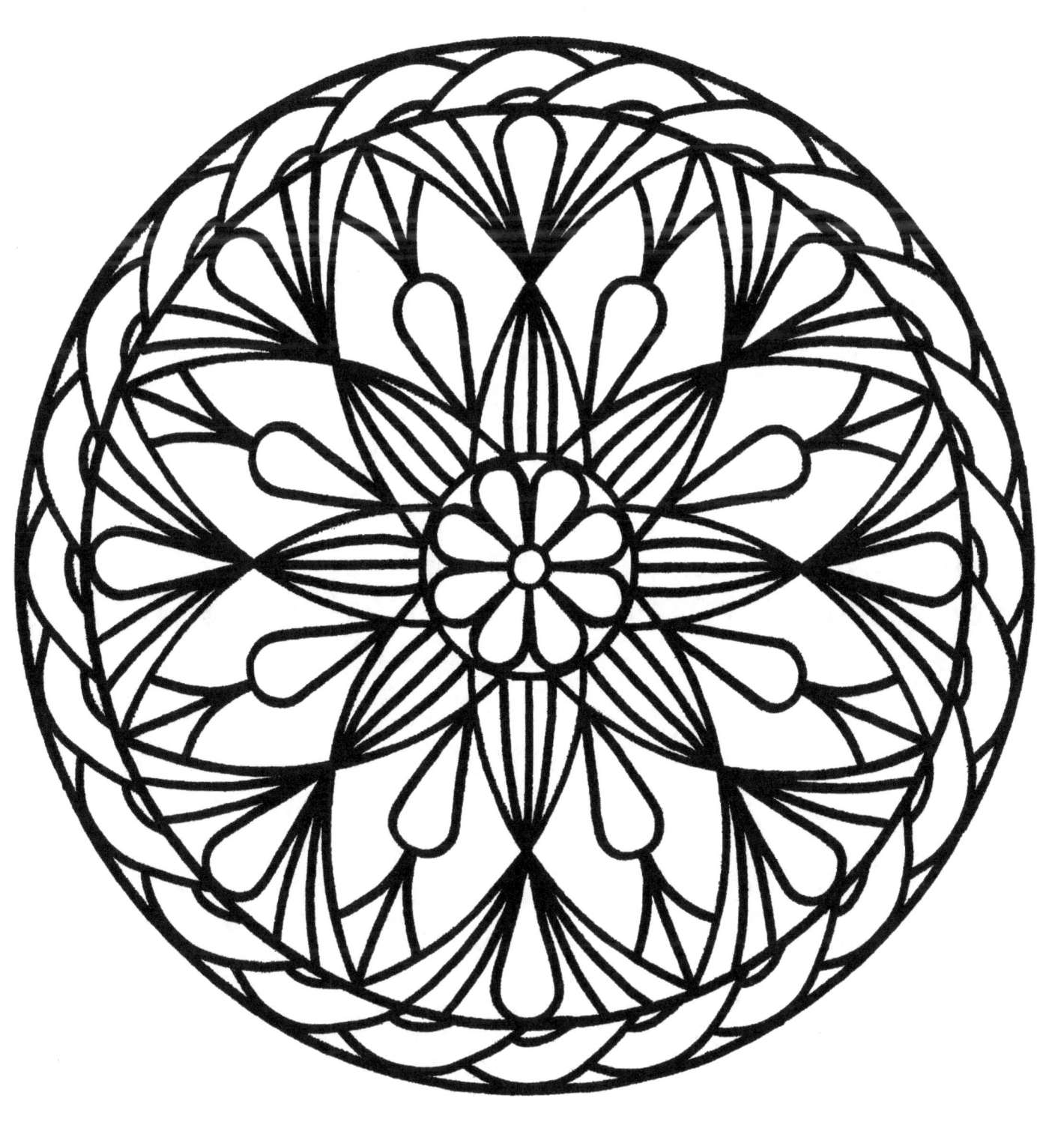

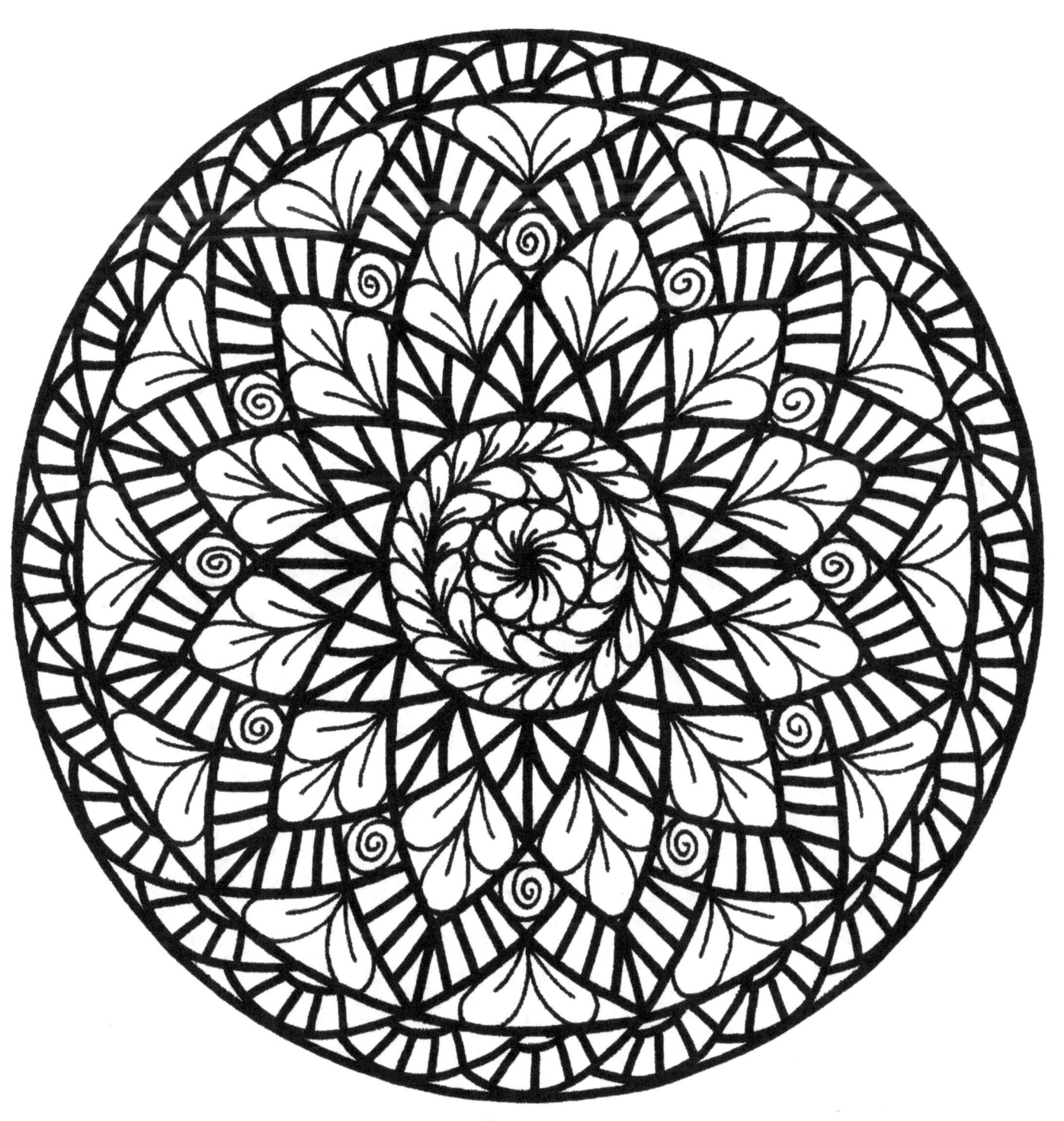

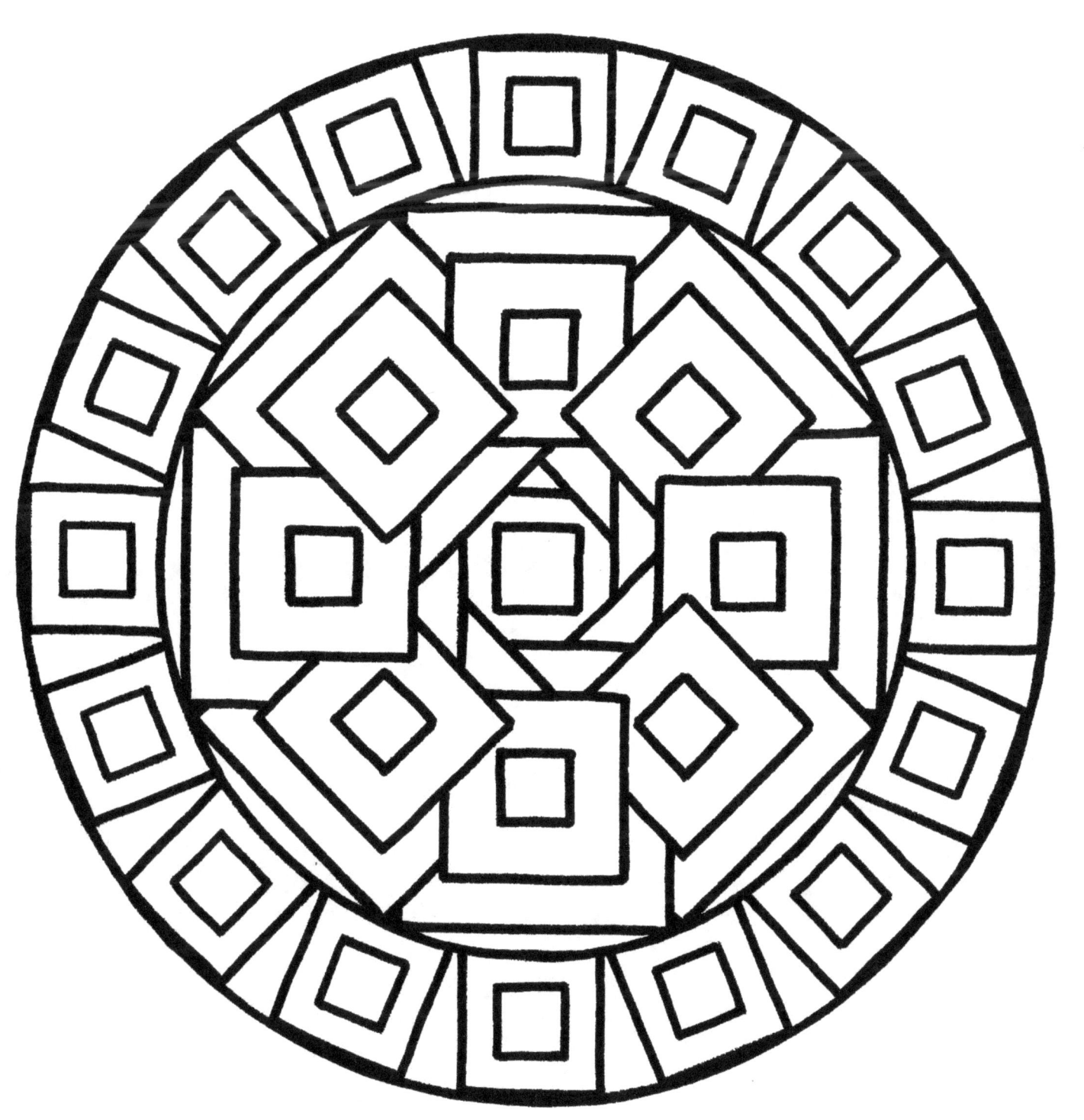

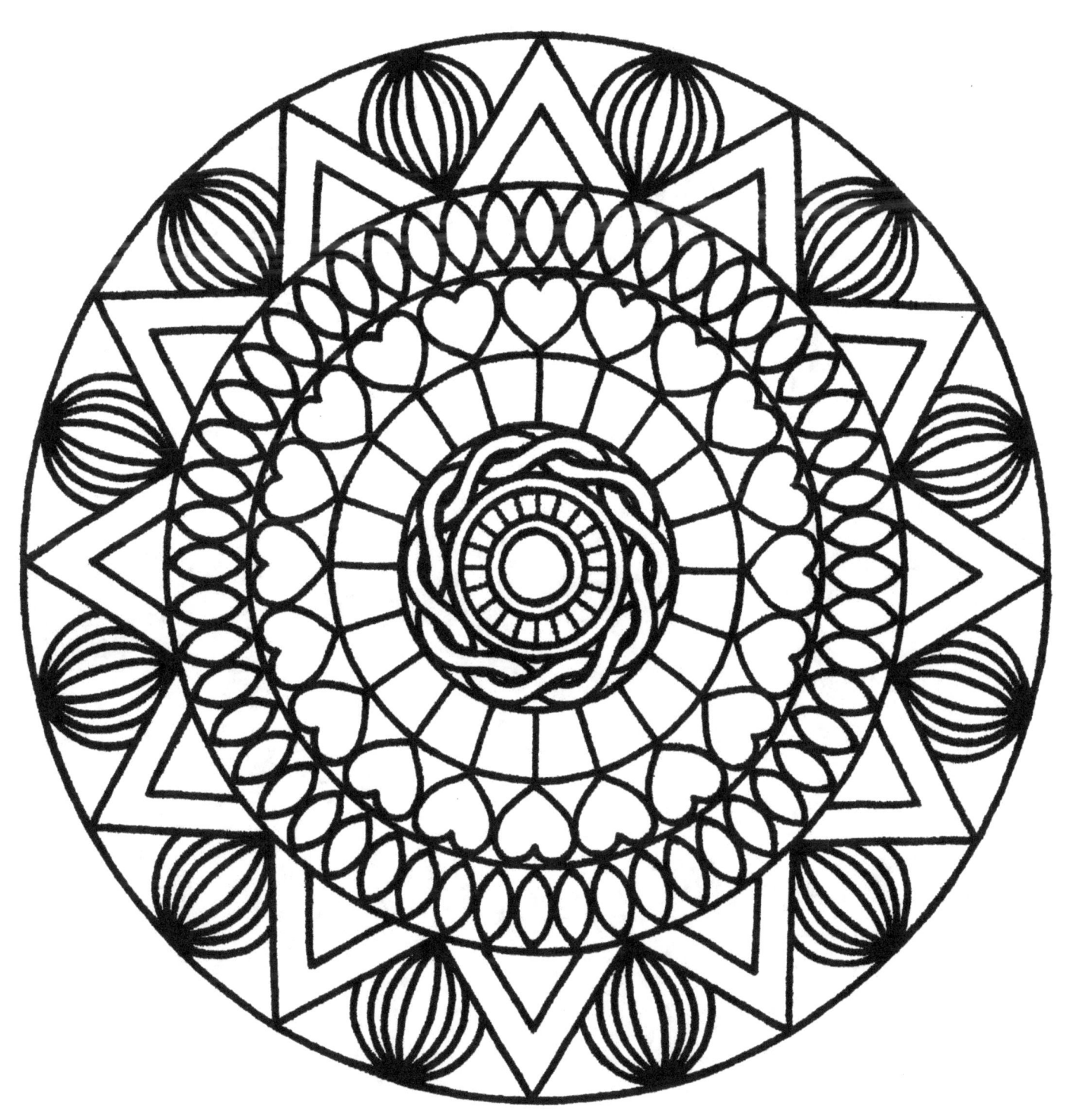

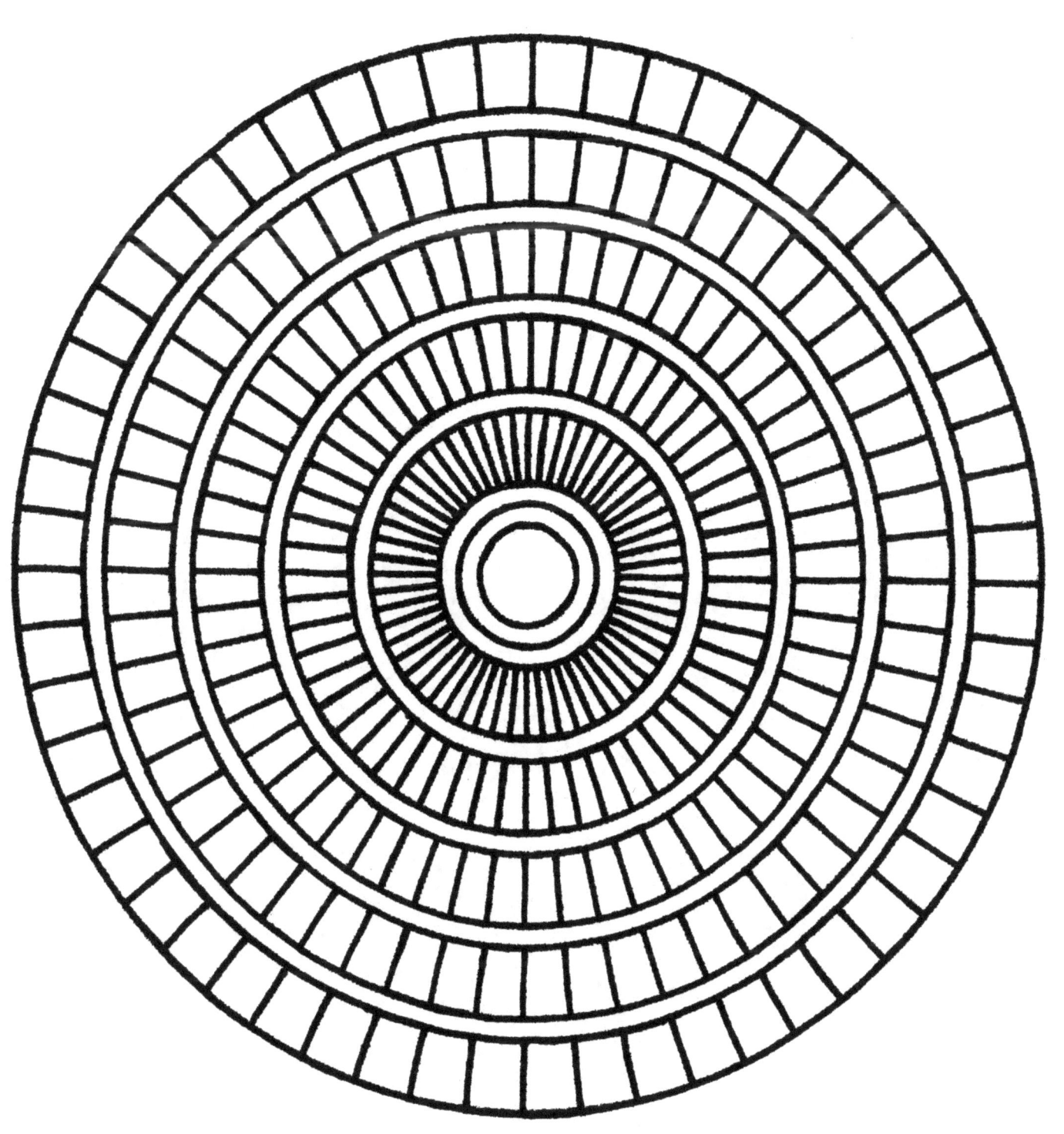

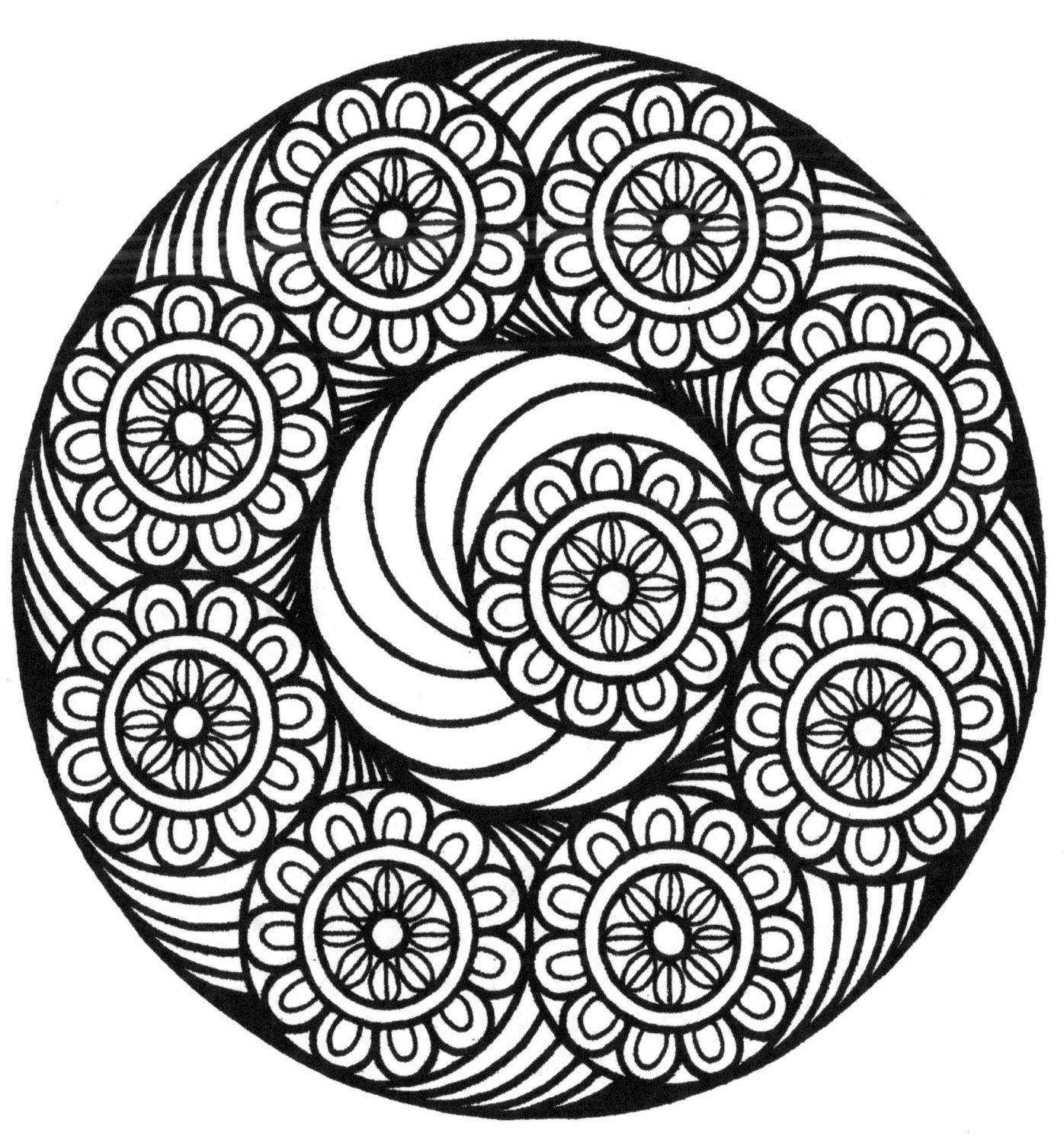

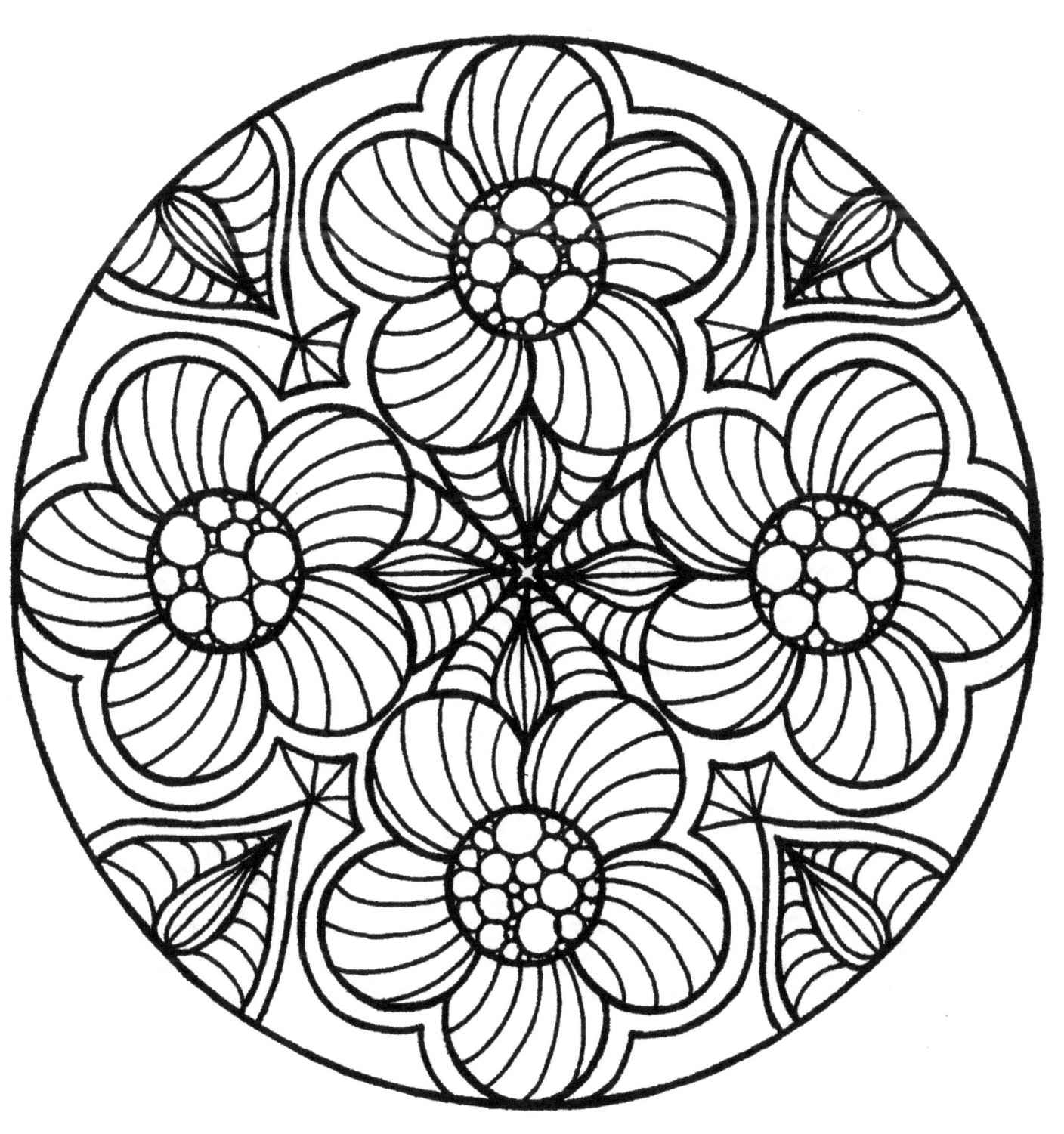

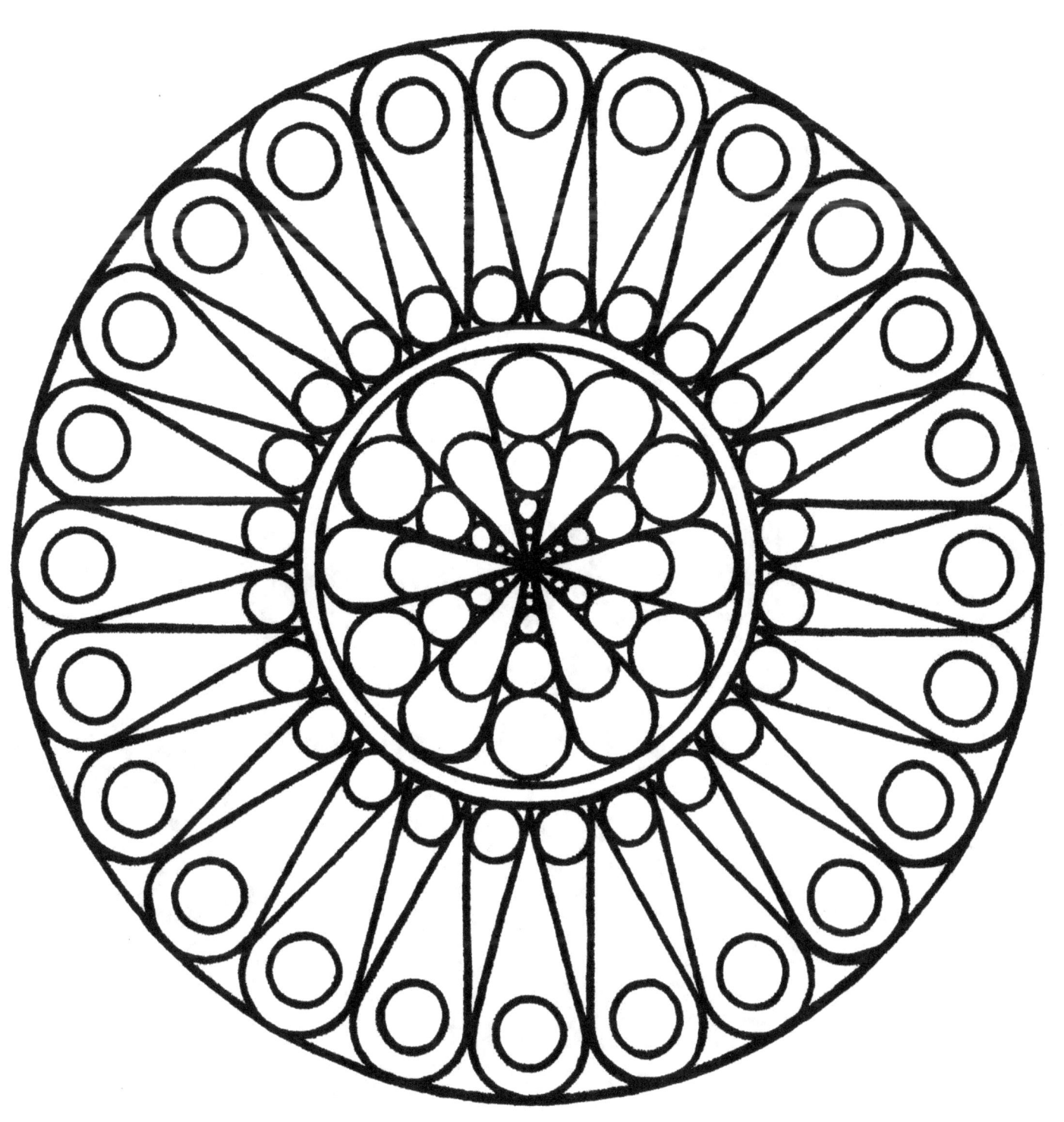

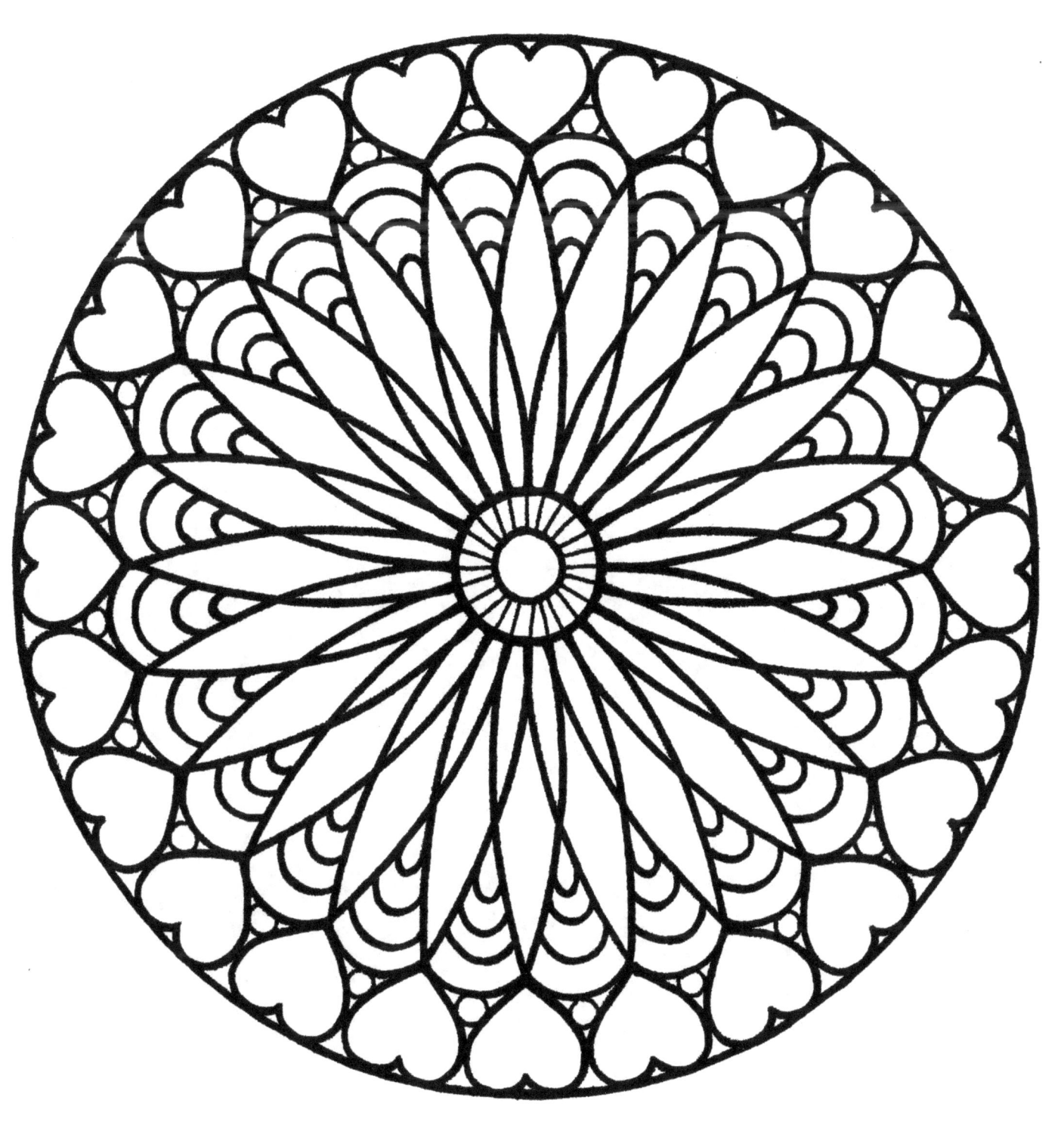

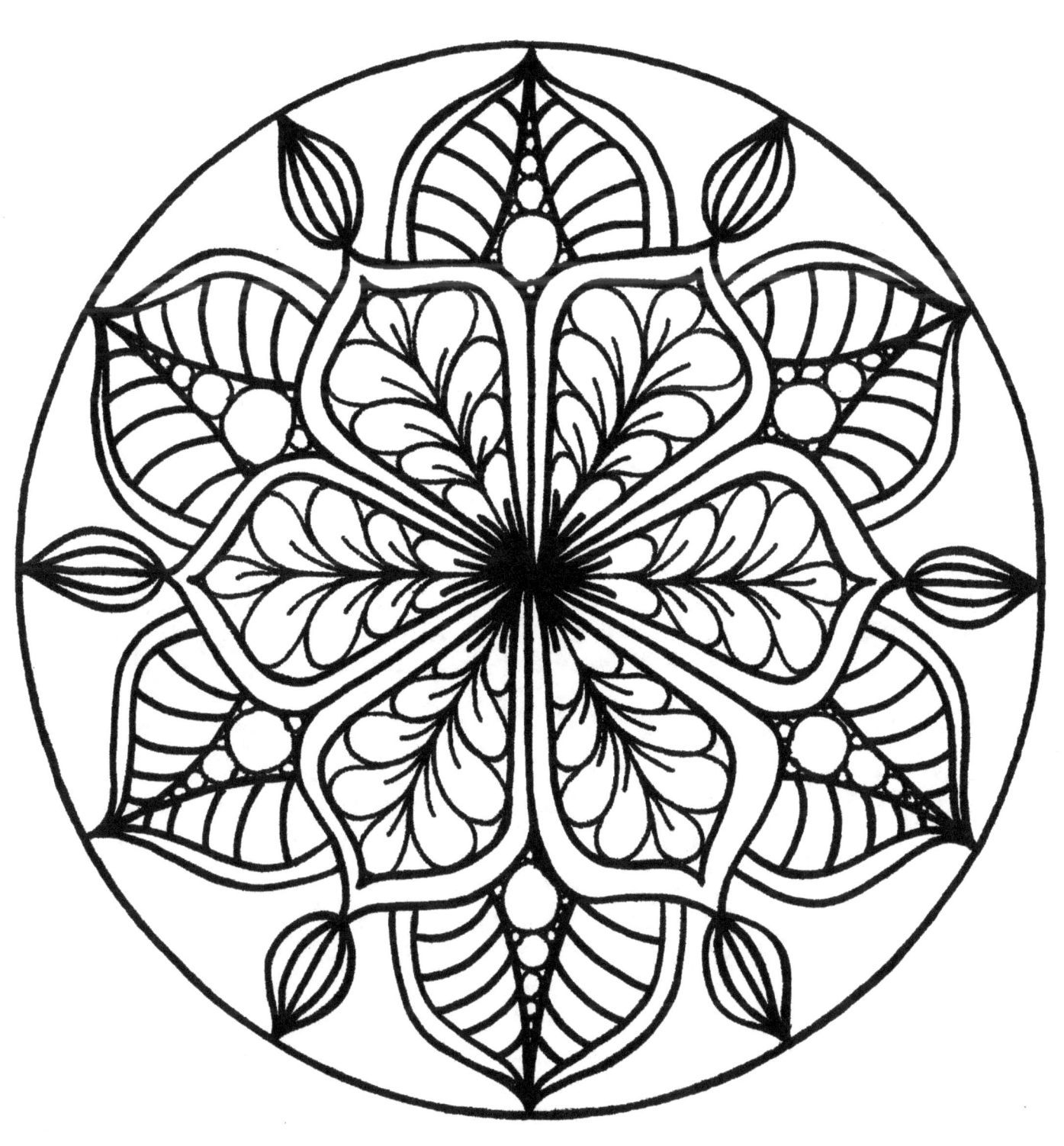

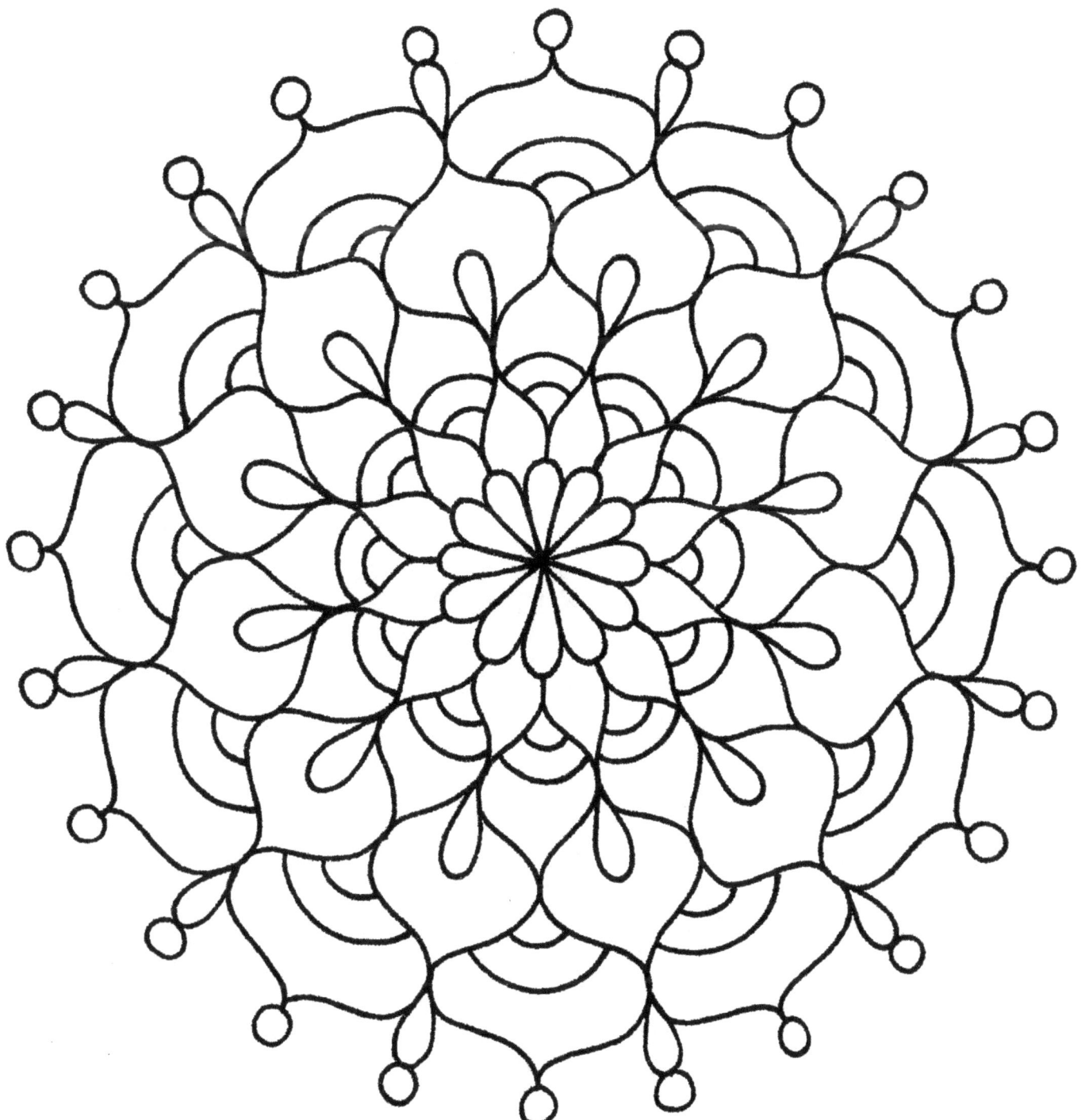

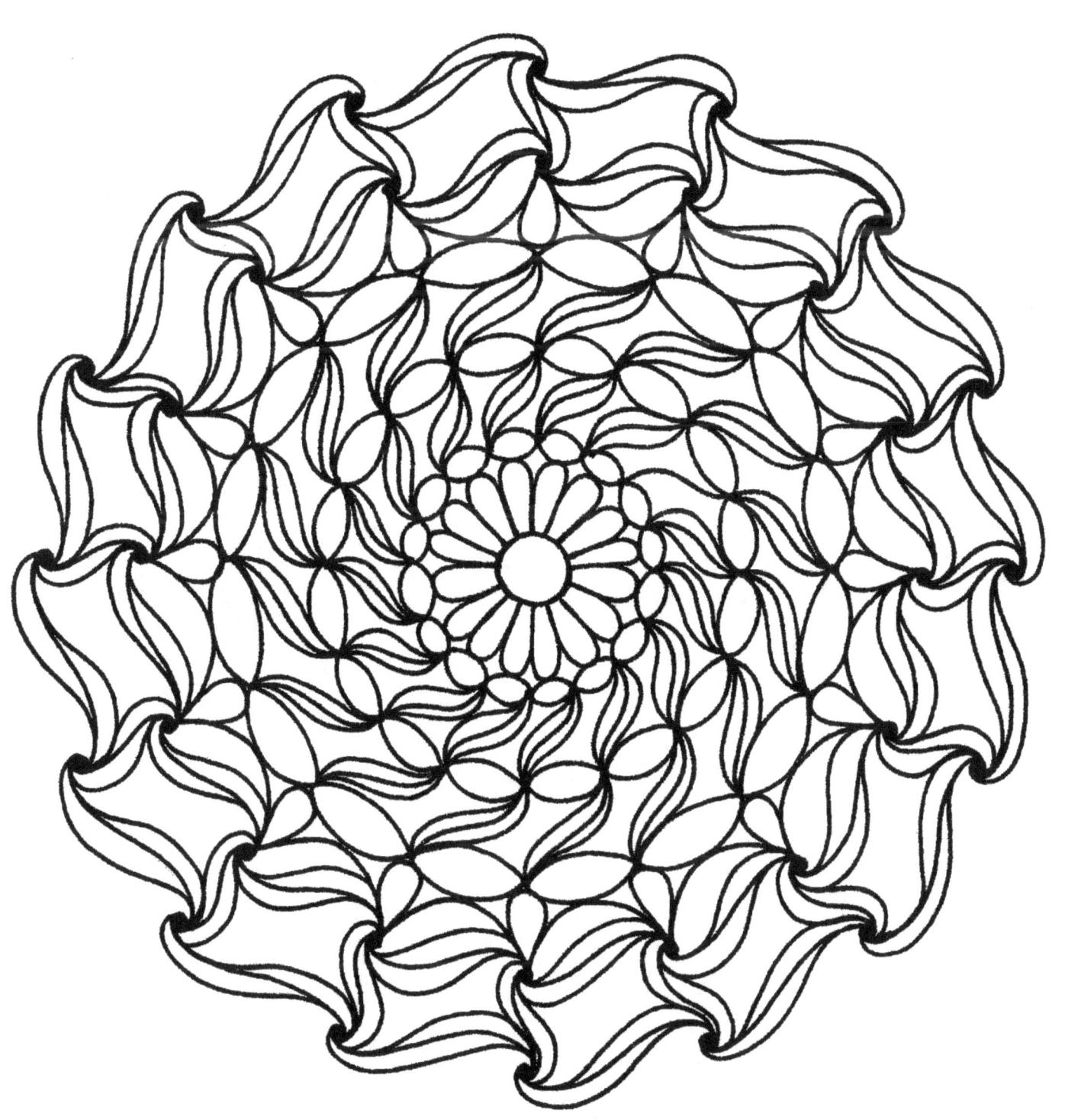

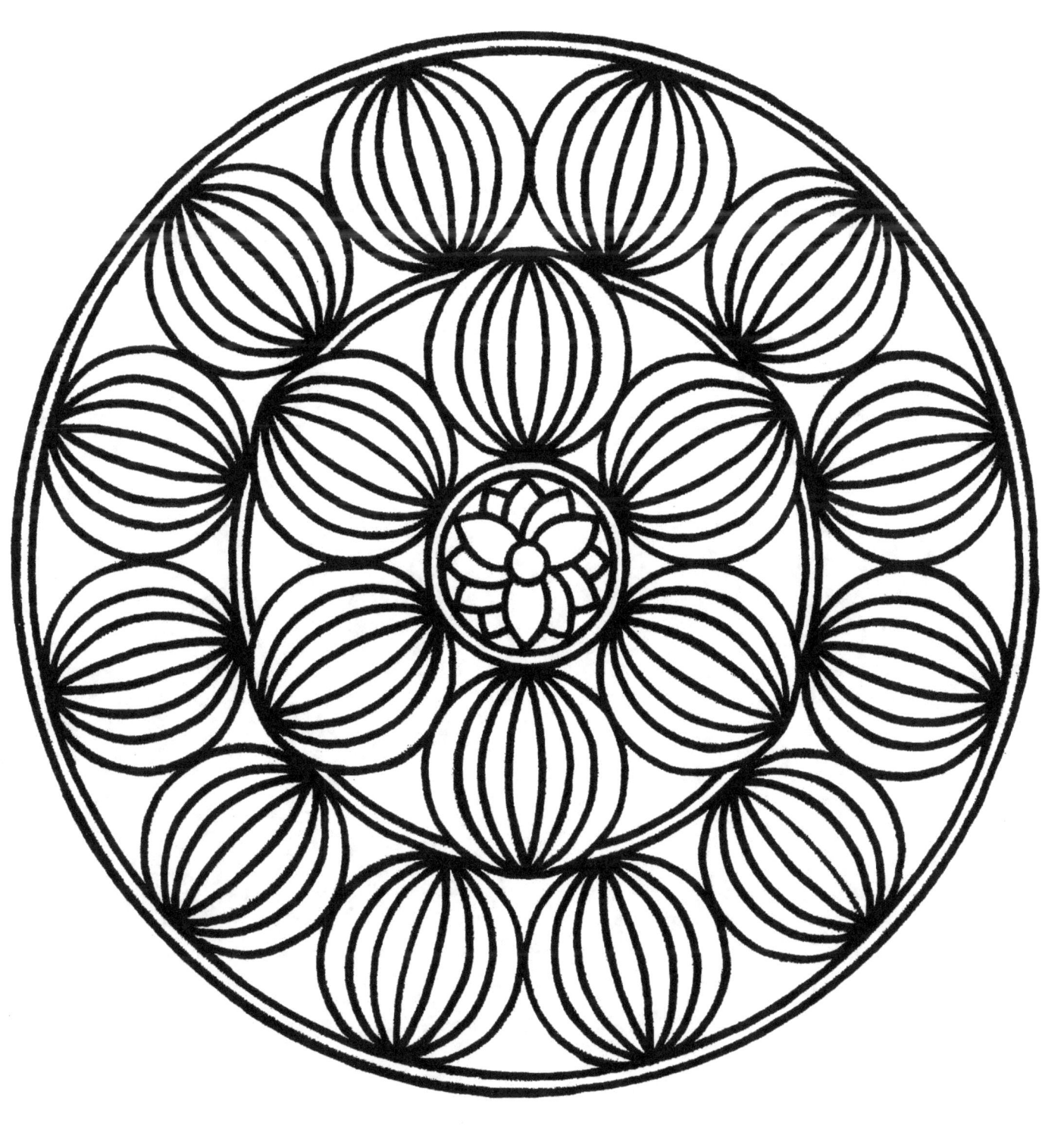

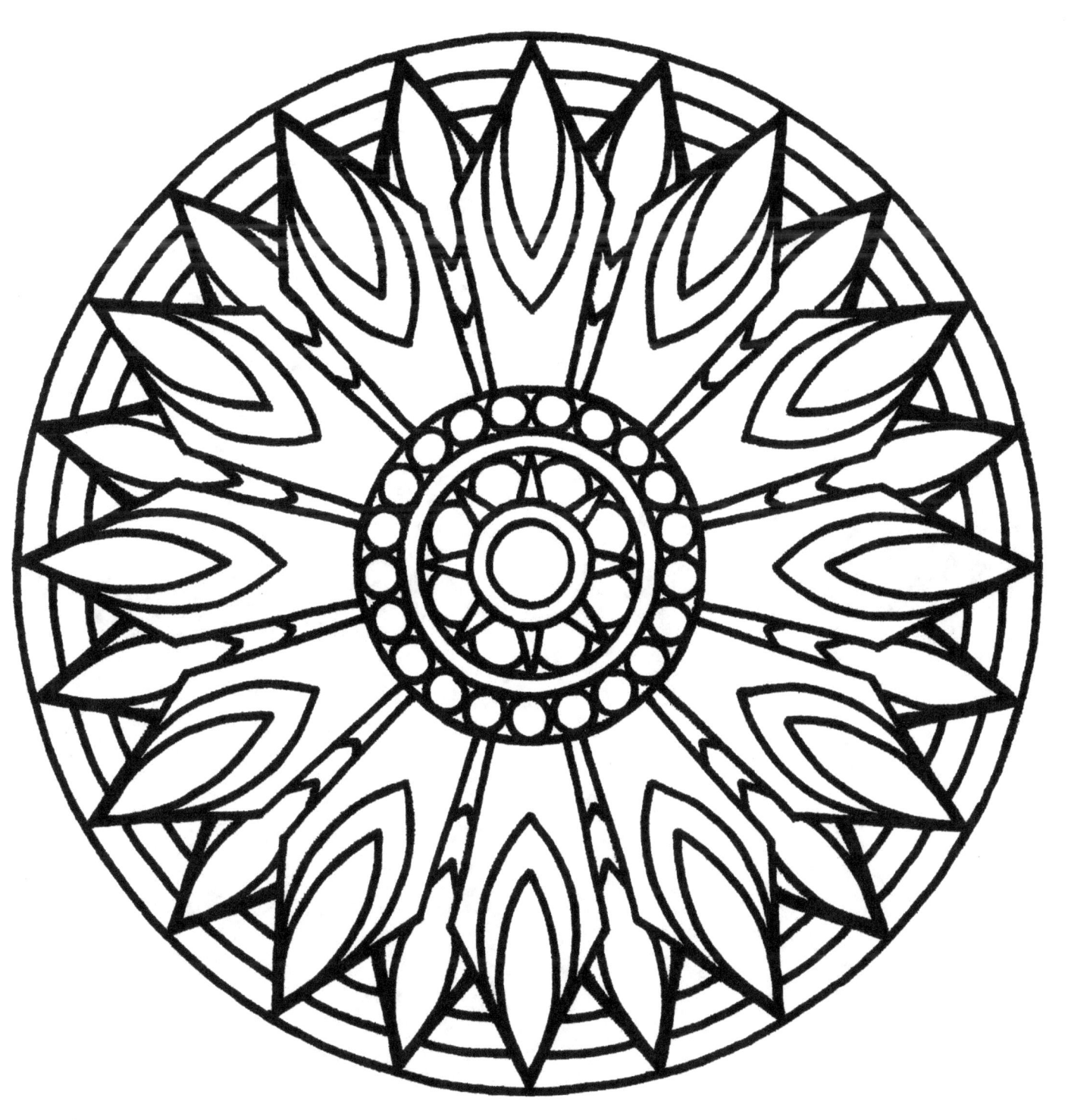

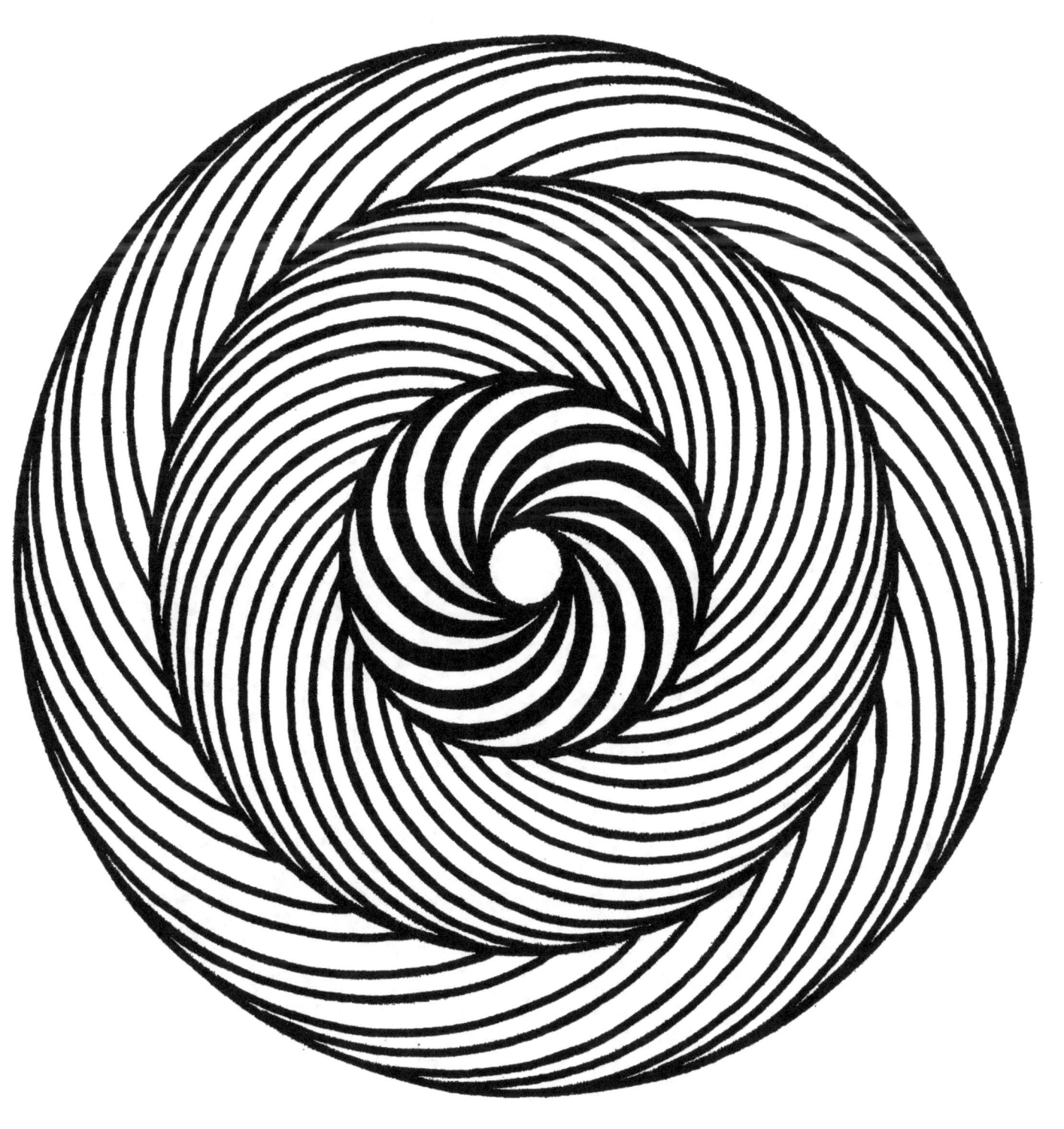

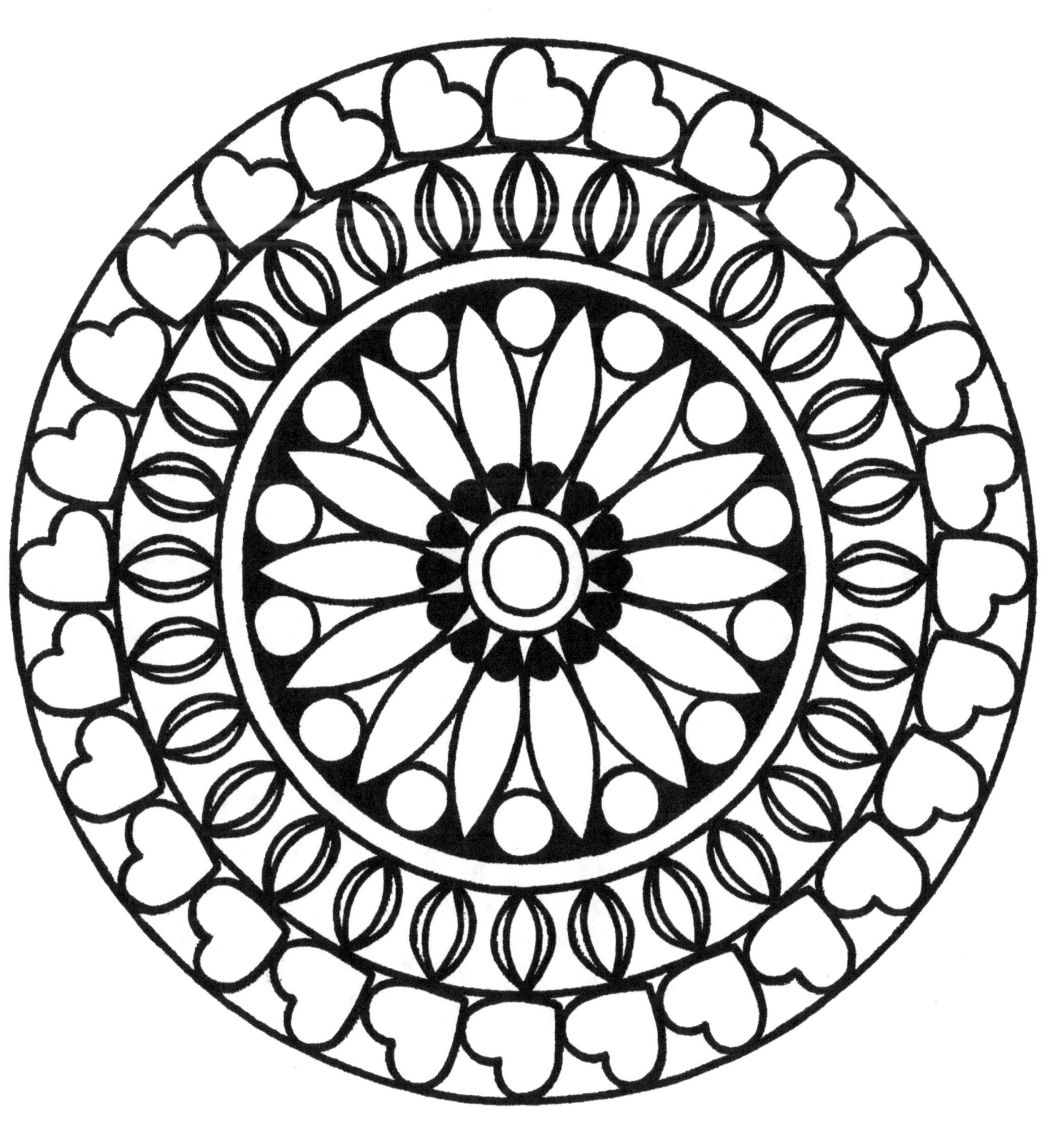

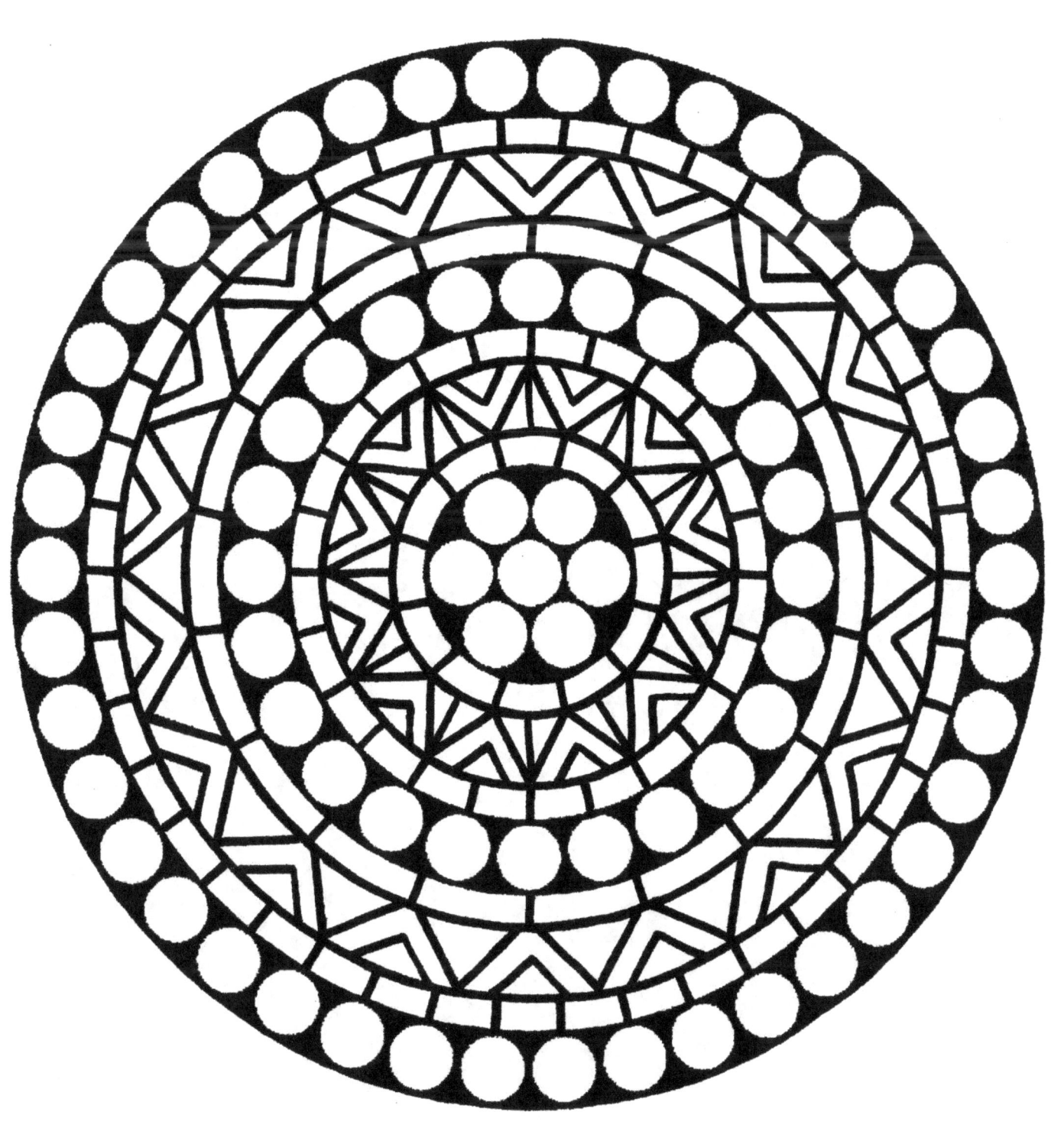

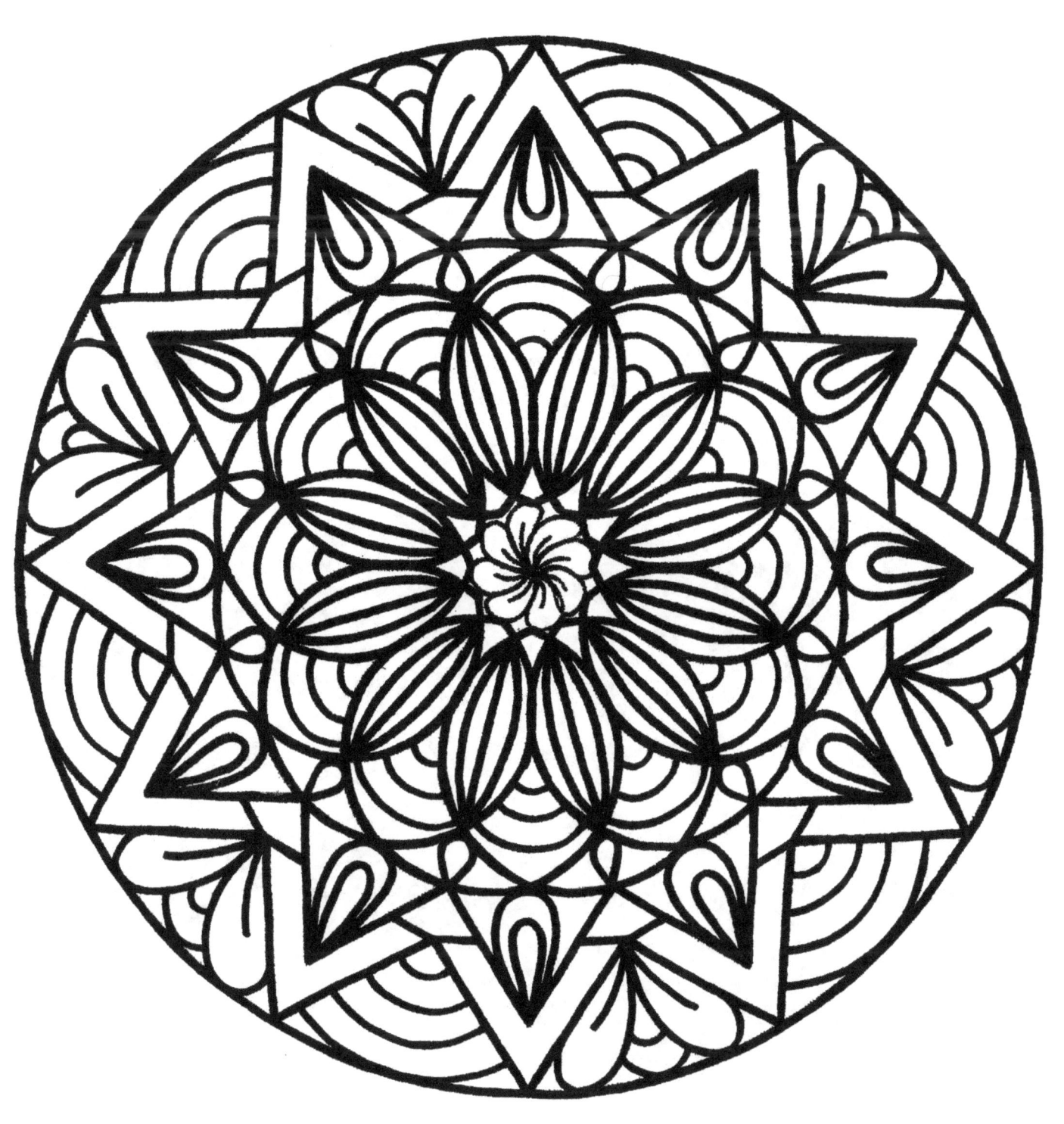

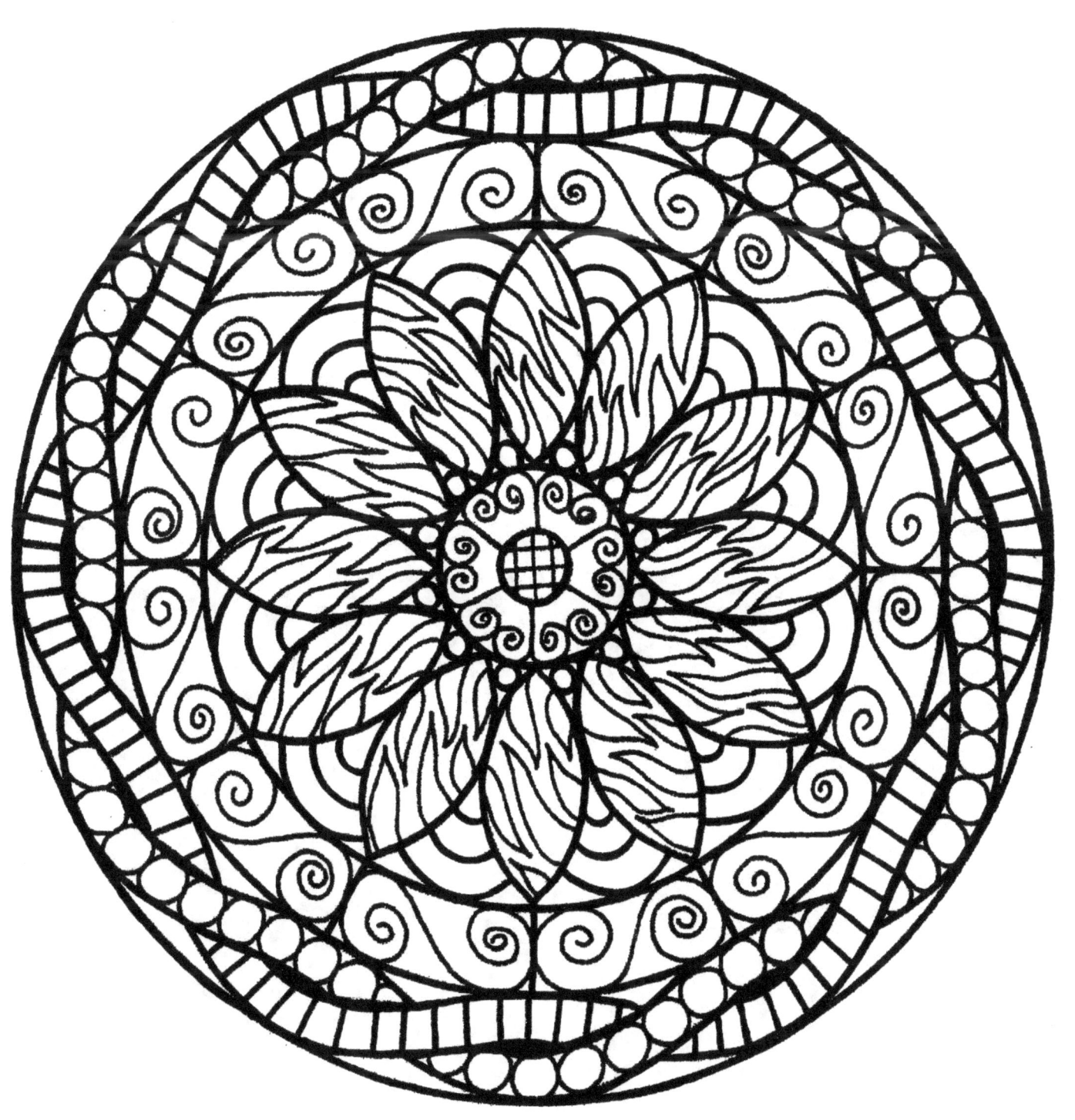

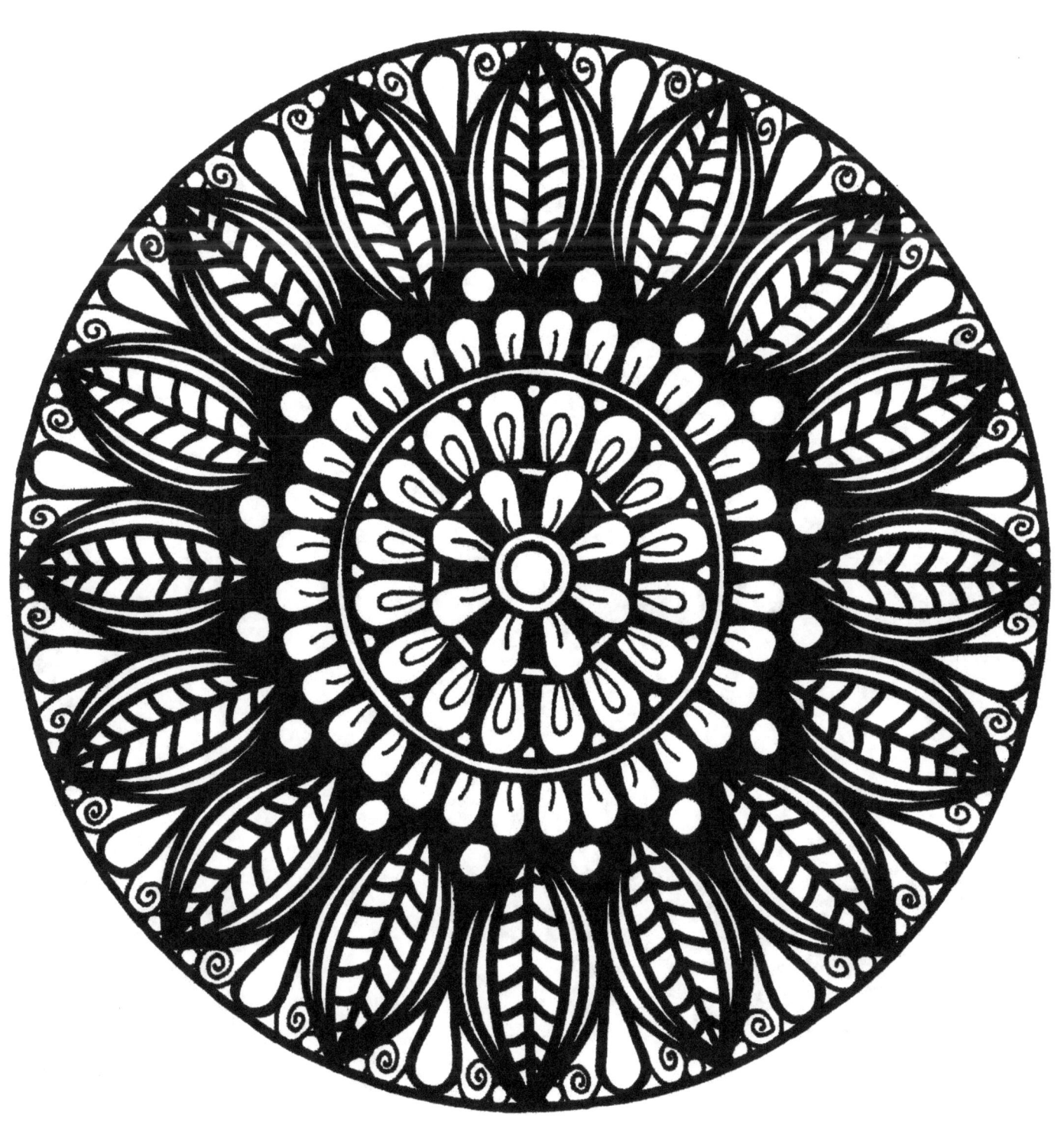

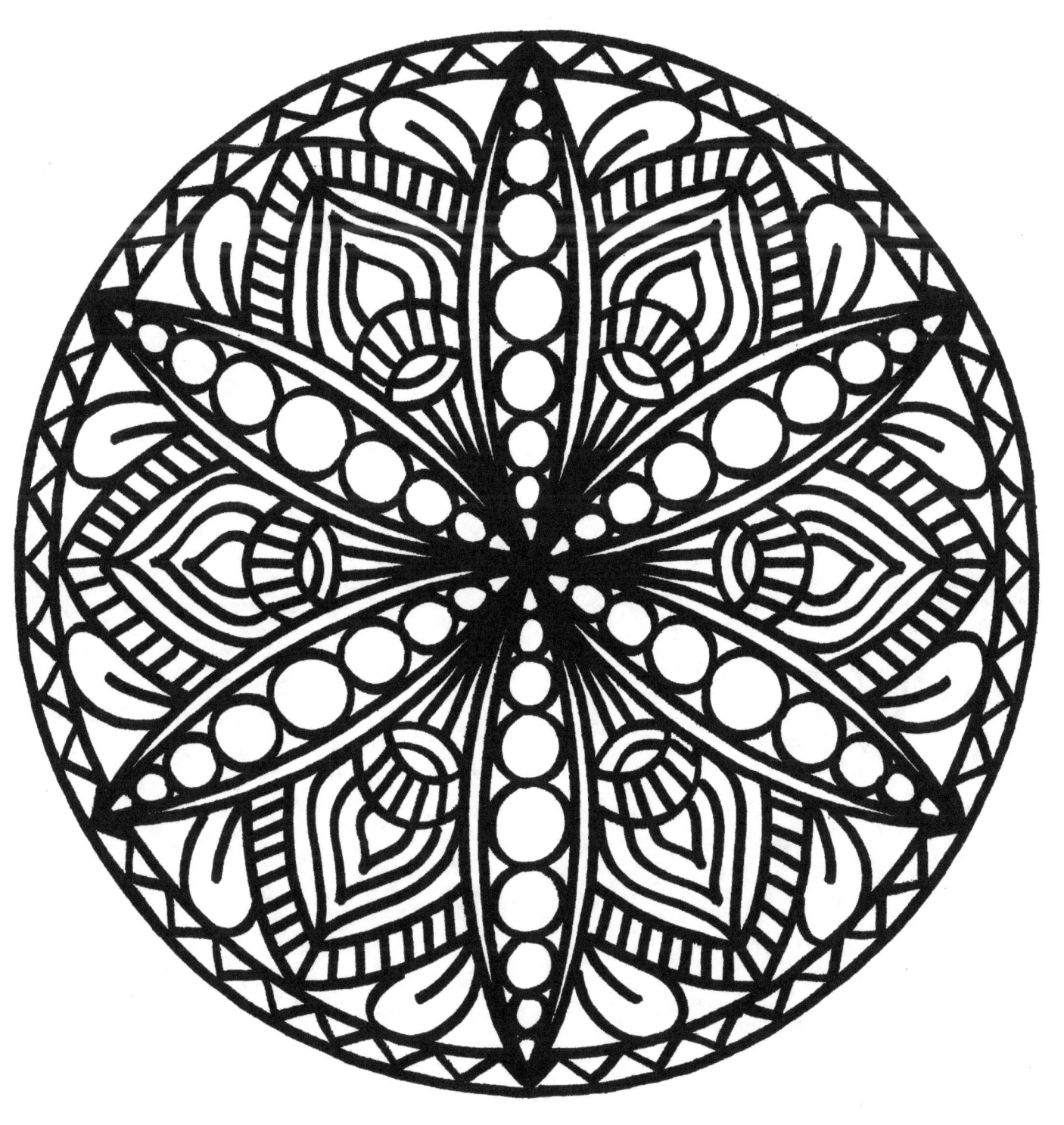

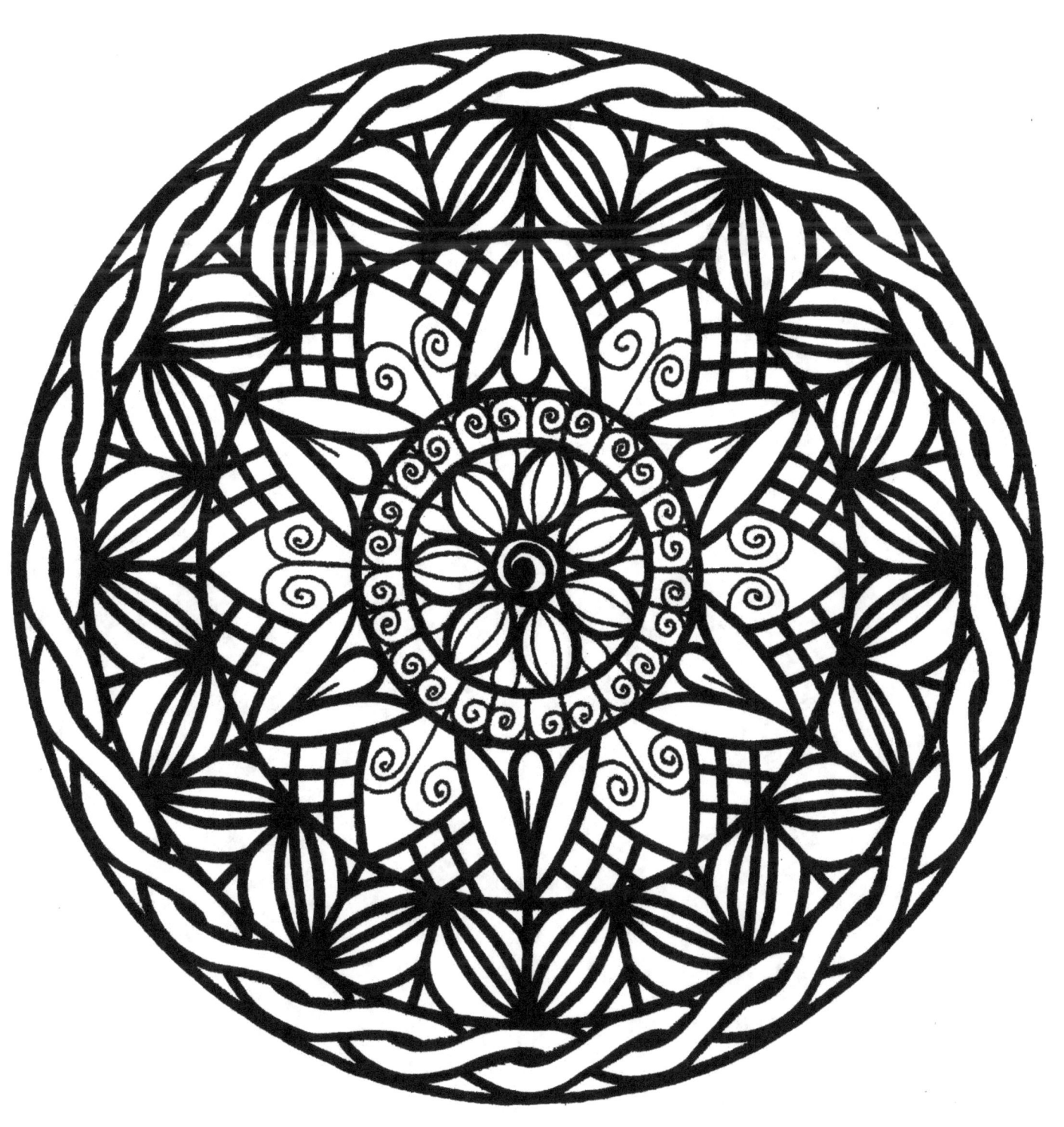

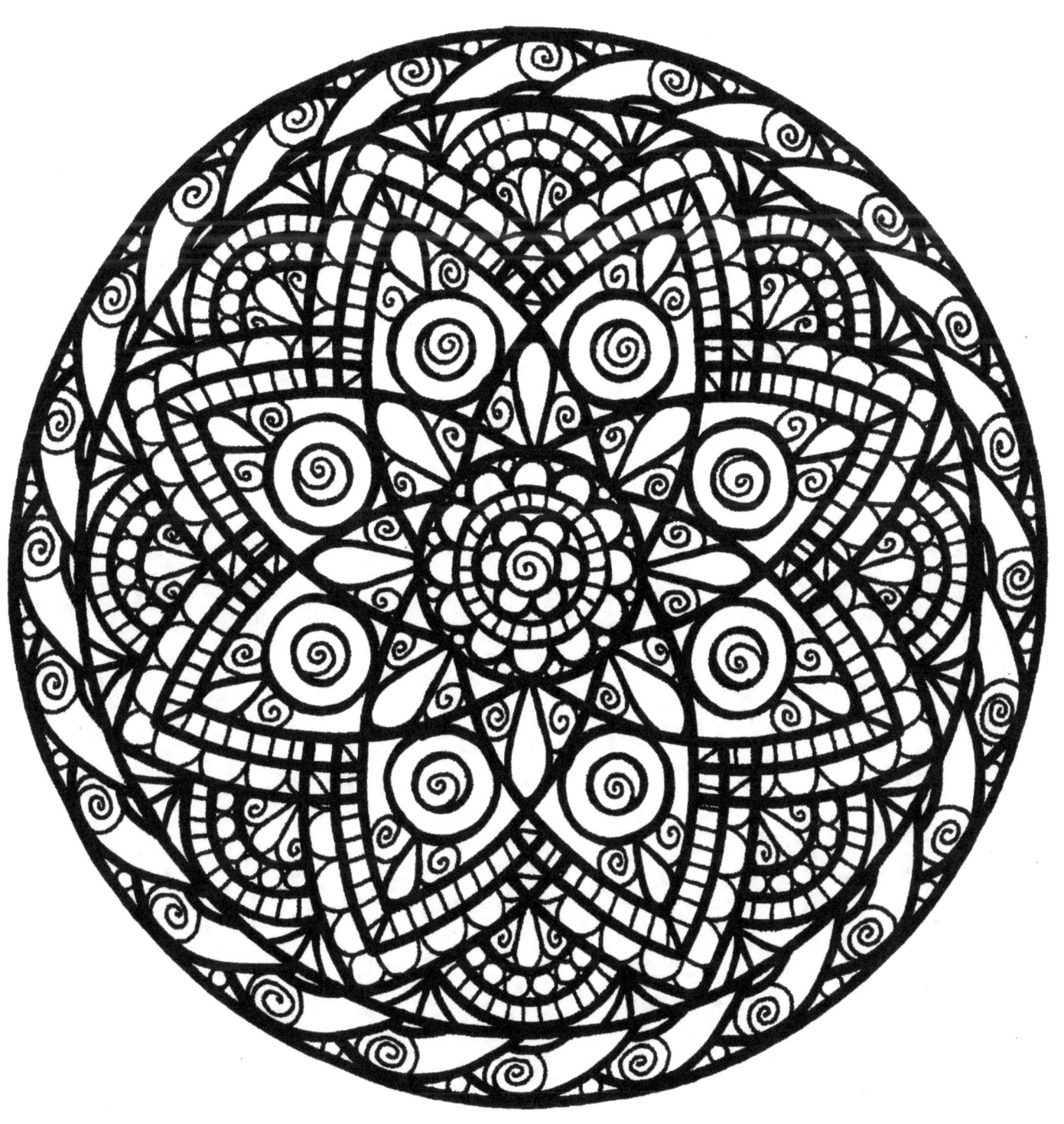

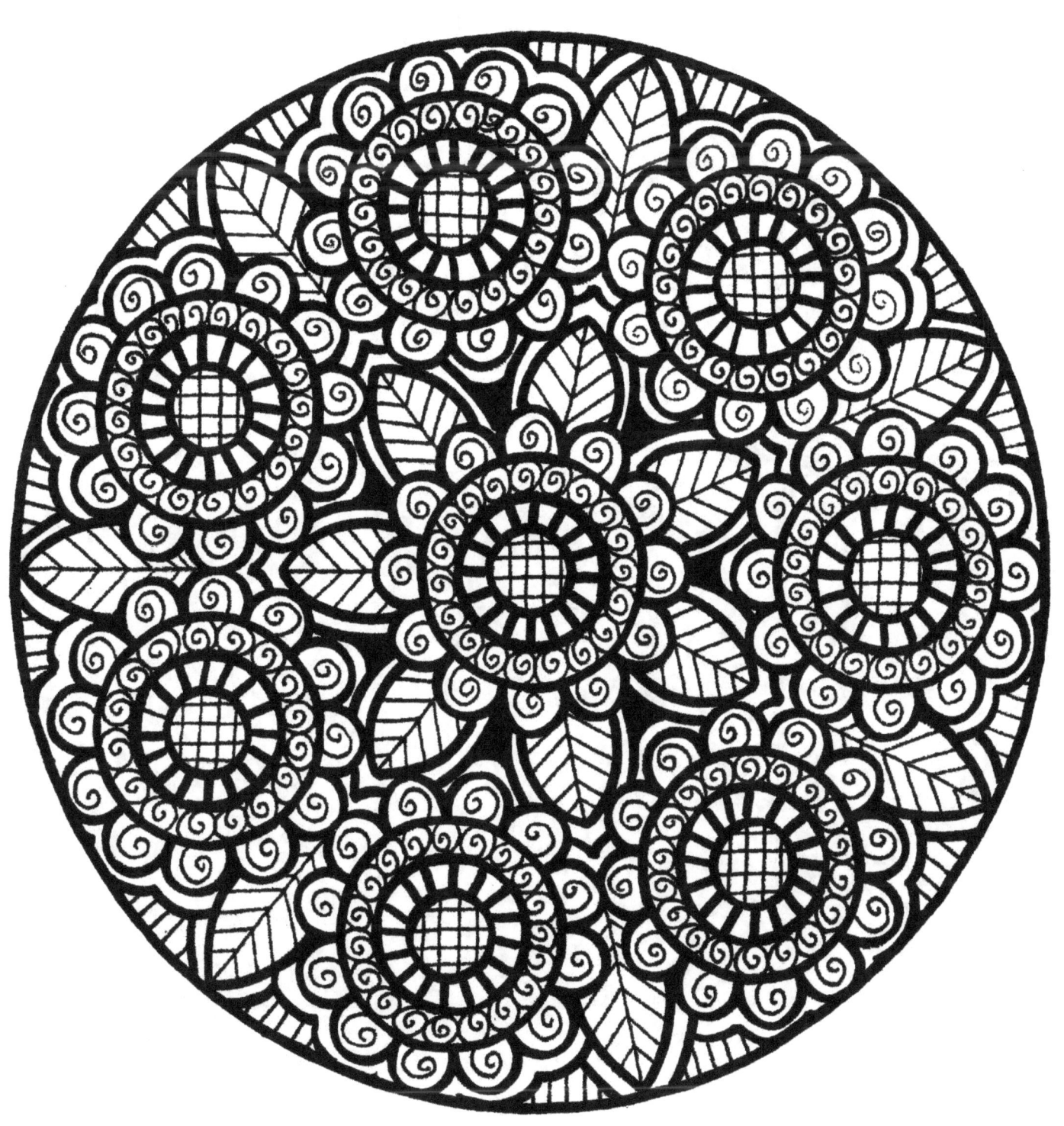

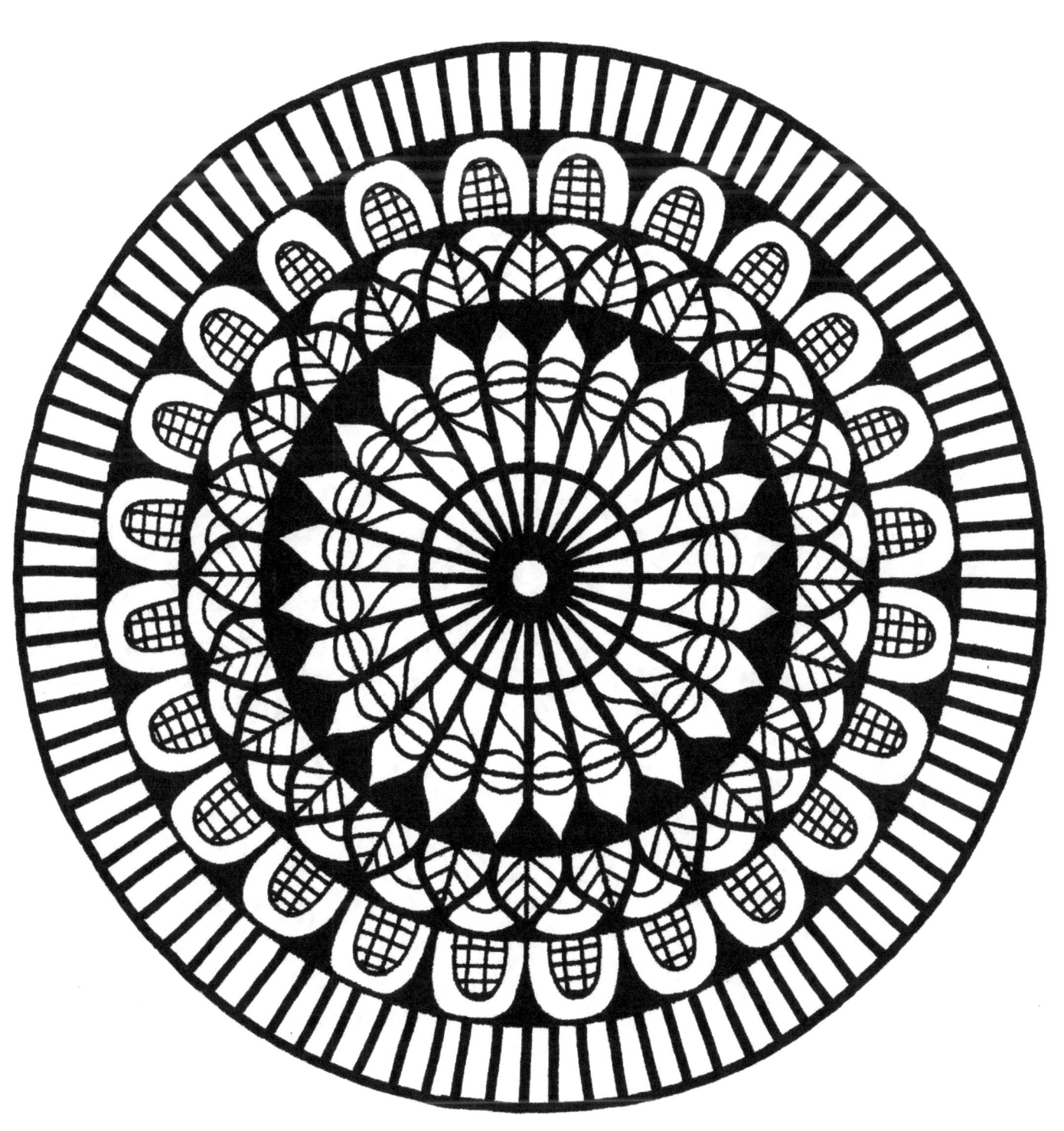

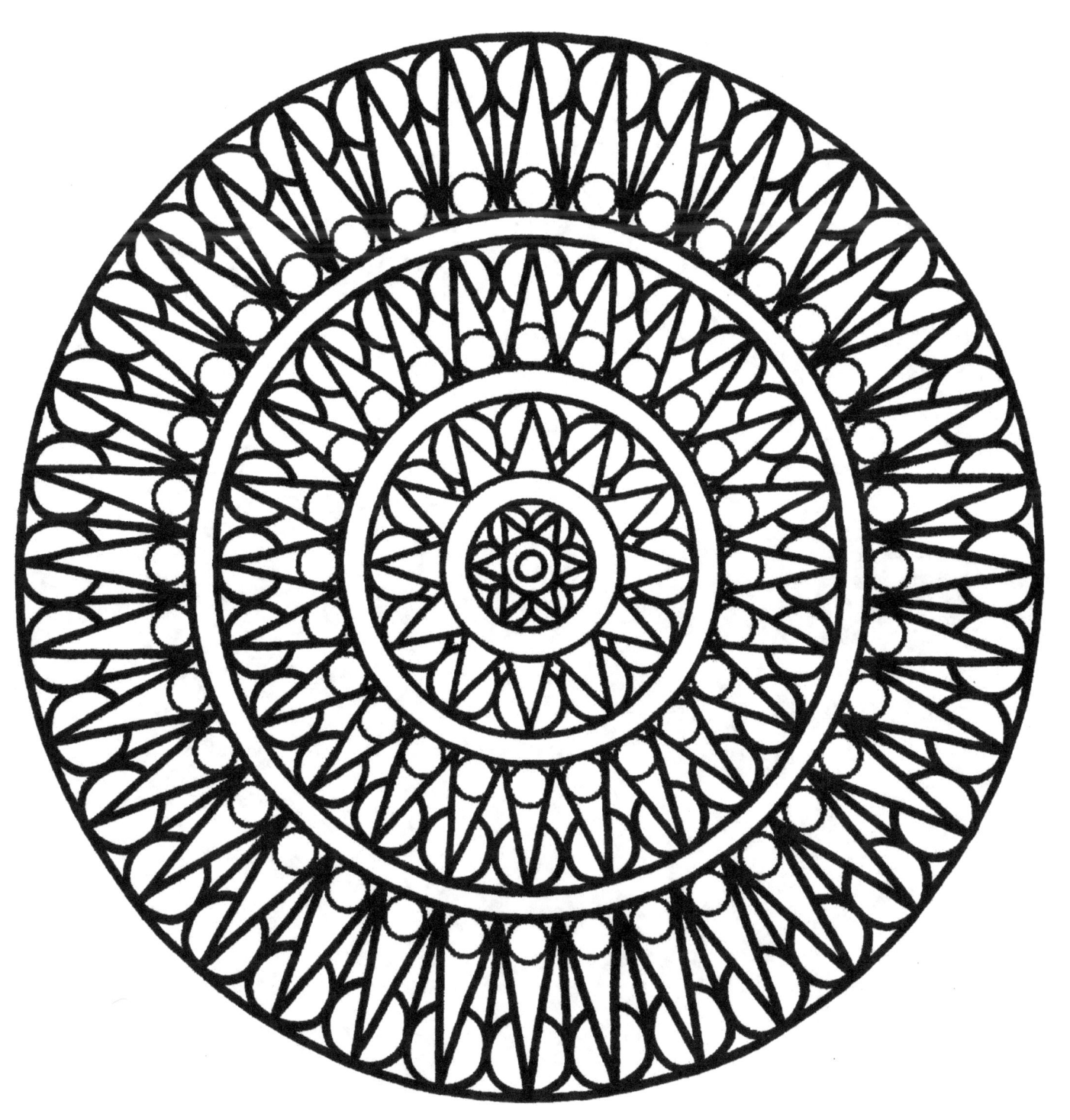

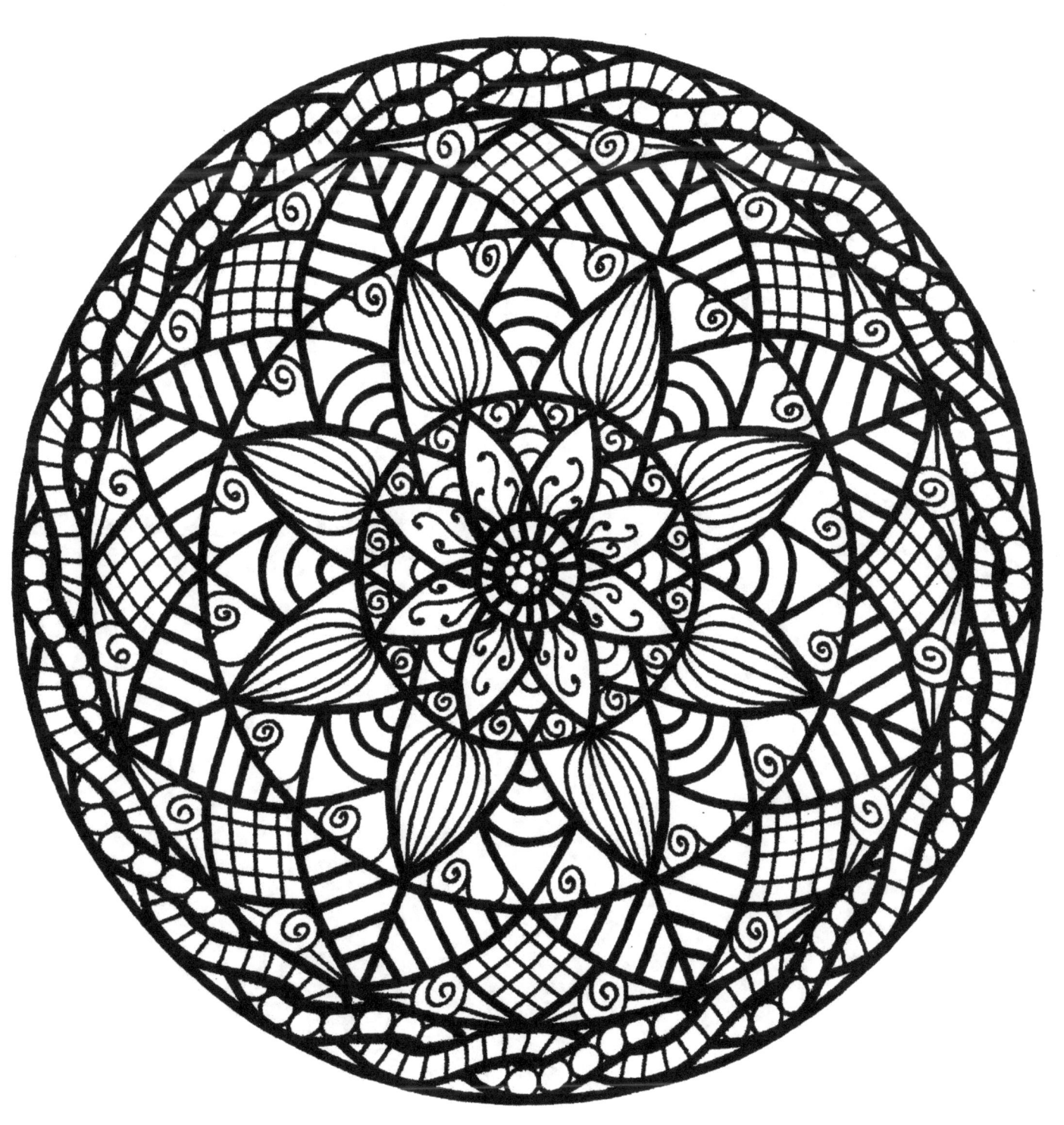

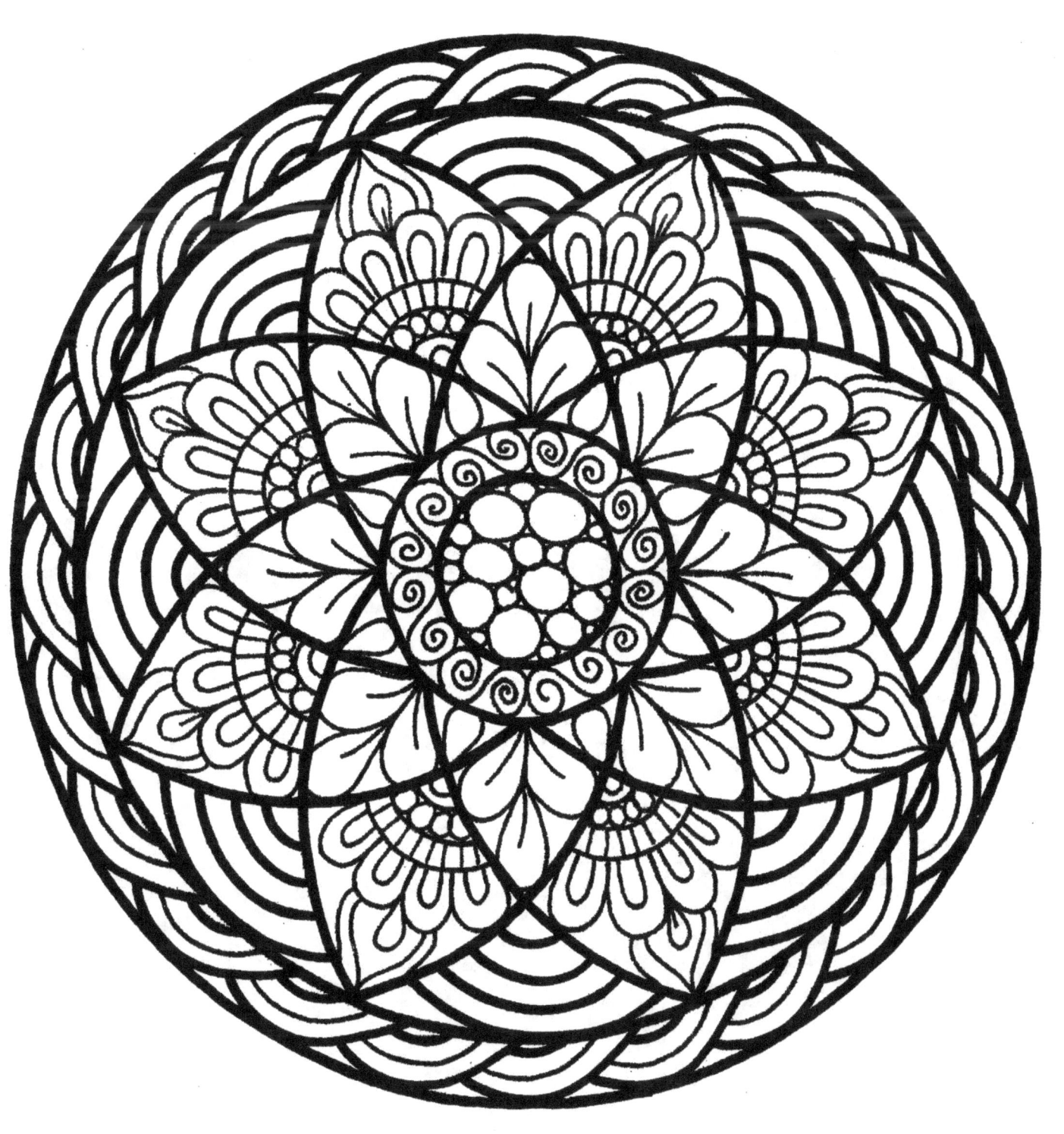

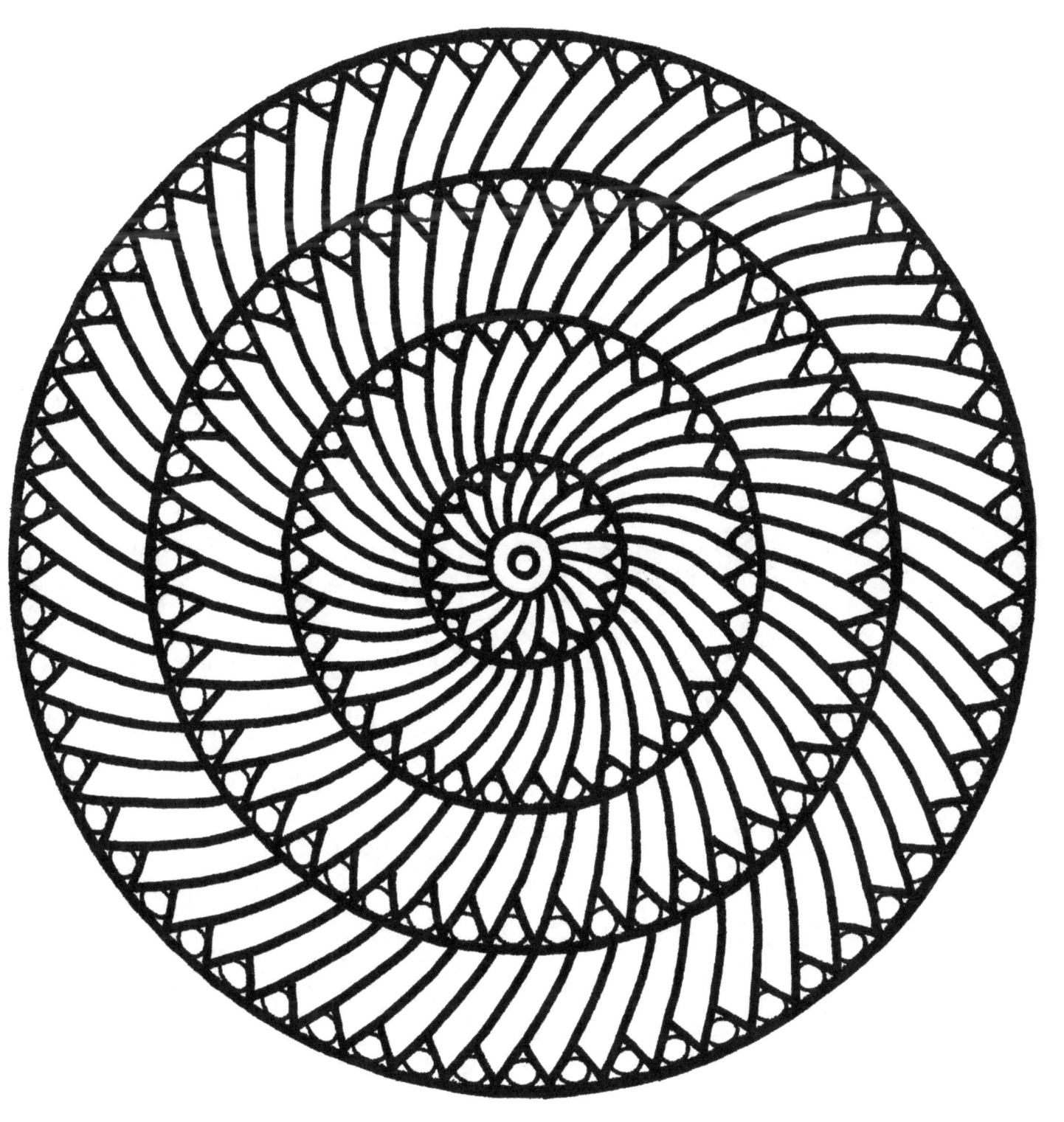

Additional Coloring Books

By Artist

Dwyanna Stoltzfus

Beautiful Circles Coloring Book

Beautiful Circles Mini Coloring Book

Beautiful Circles 2 Coloring Book

Doodle Fun Coloring Book

Doodle Fun Mini Coloring Book